history at source

RUSSIA *1914-1941*

John Laver

Hodder & Stoughton

A MEMBER OF THE HODDER HEADLINE GROUP

ACKNOWLEDGEMENTS

The cover illustration is a poster by Alexei Radakov from 1920 which was part of a state campaign against illiteracy. The caption reads:
'He who is illiterate is like a blind man. Failure and misfortune lie in wait for him on all sides'.

The Publishers would like to thank the following for permission to reproduce material in this volume:

Cambridge University Press for the extract from *Red Petrograd* by S Smith (1985); Harper Collins Publishers Ltd/Atheneum Publishers, an imprint of Macmillan Publishing Company for the extract from *Hope Against Hope* by Nadezhda Mandelstam, copyright © 1970 by Atheneum Publishers; History Today for the extract from 'Filling in the Blank Spots in Soviet History' by Yuri Afansyer from *History Today*, February 1989, London School of Economics and Political Science for the extract from Soviet Communism: *A New Civilisation* by S & B Webb (1947); Penguin Books Ltd for two extracts from *An Economic History of the USSR* by Alec Nove (Penguin Books, Revised Edition, 1989) copyright © Alec Nove, 1969, 1976, 1982, 1989; Progress Publishers for the extracts from *History of the USSR* by Y Kukushkin (1981); Random Century Group/Little Brown & Company Publishers for the extract from *Children of the Arbat* by A Rybakov (1989); Routledge for the extract from *Soviet Economic Development Since 1917* by M Dobb 6th Edition (1966); F Joseph Spieler for the extract from *The Fate of The Revolution* by W Laquer (1987); Unwin Hyman Ltd for the extract from *The Russian Civil War* by E Mawdsley (1987).

Every effort has been made to trace and acknowledge ownership of copyright. The publishers will be glad to make suitable arrangements with any copyright holders whom it has not been possible to contact.

British Library Cataloguing in Publication Data
Laver, John
   Russia, 1914–41. (History at source).
   1. Soviet Union, history
   I. Title   II. Series
   947

   ISBN–0–340–54210–1

First published 1991
Impression number   10 9 8 7 6 5
Year   1998 1997 1996

© 1991 John Laver

Printed in Great Britain for Hodder & Stoughton Educational, a division of Hodder Headline Plc, 338 Euston Road, London NW1 3BH by Redwood Books, Trowbridge, Wiltshire.

CONTENTS

PREFACE

In recent years there has been an increasing interest in modern Soviet history, partly as the result of rapid developments in the USSR in the Gorbachev era. There has long been a considerable body of literature on Soviet history, and it is a popular topic with students studying at A Level, AS Level, Higher Grade and beyond. It is also true that changes in the requirements of examination boards, particularly the introduction of source-based questions, coursework and personal assignments, have increased the demands on students and teachers alike.

This book is intended for students, and hopefully teachers, who are interested in a number of key topics in Soviet history and would benefit from a practical complement to existing textbooks and monographs. A number of central issues and topics are introduced through collections of primary and secondary sources, together with questions of the type likely to be encountered in examinations or other exercises involving use of sources. Practical advice is proffered on the way to approach such questions, and a specimen is included. Guidance is also offered on the approach to essay questions. Sample essay titles are given along with suggestions on relevant approaches; and again, a specimen answer is included. Finally, an analytical bibliography is intended to give guidance to teachers and students alike.

It is hoped that this collection will prove useful for students working as part of an organised course or on their own.

APPROACHING SOURCE-BASED QUESTIONS

Source-based questions have become an important part of History examinations at all levels in recent years. Students who have studied History at GCSE and Standard Grade will be used to handling various types of sources. The skills they have learned in handling evidence will continue to be applicable at a more advanced level, but there will also be more sophisticated skills to master and the sources themselves may be more demanding.

During your studies you will encounter both primary and secondary historical evidence. The distinction between the two is sometimes artificially exaggerated: all sources have their value and limitations, and it is possible to worry unnecessarily about a 'hierarchy of sources'. The important thing for the student is to feel confident in handling all sources. The majority of sources in this book are primary sources, since they are the raw material from which historians work; and they are mostly of a documentary nature, since that is the type most commonly found in examinations. However, the comments below will usually apply to *all* types of evidence, and there are some examples of secondary sources included.

When a student is faced with a piece of historical evidence, there are certain questions that he or she should always ask of that source; but in an examination that student will be asked specific questions set by an examiner and, in the light of pressures, not least of which is time, it is important to approach these questions in an organised and coherent fashion. The following advice should be borne in mind when answering source-based questions. Some of the advice may appear obvious in the cold light of day, but, as examiners will testify, the obvious is often ignored in the cauldron of the examination room!

1   Read the sources carefully before attempting to answer the questions, whether there is one source or a collection of them. This will give you an overview of the sources which will usually be connected and related to a particular theme. You will study the individual sources in detail when you answer specific questions.

2   Always look carefully at the attribution of the sources: the author and date of publication; the recipient, if any; the context in which the source was produced; all these will often give you an insight in addition to that provided by the content of the source itself.

3   Mark allocations are usually given at the end of each question or sub-question. Ignore the marks at your peril! The number of marks will almost certainly give you some indication of the length of answer expected. Length of answer is not an indicator of quality, and there is no such thing as a standard answer, but it is commonplace for candidates in examinations to write paragraph-length answers to questions carrying one or two marks. A question carrying such a low mark can usually be adequately answered in two or three sentences. You do not have the time to waste your purple prose in examinations! Similarly, a mark allocation of nine or ten marks indicates the expectation of a reasonably substantial answer.

4   Study the wording of the questions very carefully. Some questions will ask you to use *only* your own knowledge in the answer; some will ask you to use *both* your own knowledge *and* the source(s); some will insist that you confine your answer to knowledge gleaned from the source(s) *alone*. If you ignore the instructions, you will certainly deprive yourself of marks.

5   If there are several sources to be consulted, ensure that you make use of the ones to which you are directed – candidates have been known to ignore some or choose the wrong ones.

6   Certain types of question require a particular type of response:

a)   Comparison of sources: ensure that you do compare all the sources referred to in the question.

b)   Testing the usefulness and limitations of sources: if you are asked to do both, ensure that you do consider both aspects. You may be required to evaluate a source in relation to other information provided, or in the context of your own background knowledge of the subject.

c)   Testing reliability: this is not the same as considering the utility of a source, although students sometimes confuse the two concepts.

d)   Phrases such as 'Comment upon', 'Analyse' or 'Assess': ensure that you do what is asked. Do not be afraid of quoting extracts from a source in your answer, but avoid over-quotation or too much direct paraphrasing, since questions will usually be testing more than comprehension. You should therefore simply be illustrating or amplifying a particular point. Always *use* the sources and do not just regurgitate what is in front of you.

e)   Synthesis: this is a high-level skill which requires you to blend several pieces of evidence and draw general conclusions.

7   If at all possible, avoid spending too much time on the sources questions in examinations. Frequently candidates answer the sources questions thoroughly but do not allow themselves enough time to do justice to the rest of the examination paper, and essay answers sometimes suffer in consequence if they are attempted last.

8   If possible, read published examiners' reports which will give you further indication as to the most useful approaches to particular questions, and the pitfalls to avoid.

A Note on this Collection of Sources

It is the intention of this collection to give ideas to teachers and realistic examples of sources and questions to students, either for use in schools and colleges or for self-study purposes. However, they are intended to be flexible. If it is found helpful, adapt the questions or mark allocations, or devise new questions; or use the sources as part of coursework or personal studies. You might even find it an interesting exercise to put together your own sources and appropriate questions.

1 THE POLITICAL AND ECONOMIC SITUATION OF RUSSIA IN 1914

The political stability of the Tsarist system of government and the health of the Russian economy by 1914 have long been controversial issues amongst Soviet and non-Soviet historians.

Taking the political situation first, it is quite clear that the Tsarist regime had survived the crisis of the 1905 Revolution, and that concessions such as the establishment of the Duma, or parliamentary system, had not fundamentally weakened the theoretical power of the autocracy. On the other hand, there were danger signs: notably a revival of popular discontent after 1912 amongst the expanding proletariat or working class, demonstrated by an increasing number of strikes. The peasantry appeared more quiescent, possibly in part as a result of Stolypin's agricultural reforms, but also because they were less easy to motivate and organise politically. Perhaps more potentially dangerous was the fact that other classes were beginning to reveal their own grievances: members of the aristocracy whose economic and political influence had steadily declined since the mid-nineteenth century and who could not be relied upon to back the autocracy in all circumstances; the middle classes whose numbers grew as Russia industrialised but who lacked the influence of their counterparts in western constitutional states; and the intellectuals who felt alienated from the regime and provided the bulk of the leadership of the various revolutionary and liberal groupings by 1914. Nationalist movements within the Russian Empire posed another potential threat. Nicholas II failed to appreciate the growing isolation of his regime, which depended largely upon the bureaucracy and the army for its existence.

In economic terms, Russia's position in 1914 has been a subject of extended controversy. The bare facts are as follows: there had been considerable industrial expansion in the late nineteenth century as a result of Witte's policies. This was followed by a period of stagnation in the early years of this century, and then another boom period after 1909. Absolute growth rates in certain sectors of Russian industry were impressive, although Russia was starting from a low industrial base, and foreign capital remained a significant factor in the expansion. Agriculture remained a problem with its low productivity.

Would Russia have experienced significant economic growth but for the interruptions of war and revolution? It is an impossible question to answer. We can only take account of certain factors and speculate: agriculture remained a problem; the concentration of an expanding working class in urban centres was a potential source of unrest; many features of Russia's industries were backward by contemporary standards. Yet considerable progress had been achieved in some areas. Therefore the arguments are likely to continue.

A Growth Indices of Some Industries in Russia 1890–1900 and 1905–1913

	1890	1900	1905	1913
Pig iron	100	314	100	169
Coal	100	269	100	193
Steel	100	586	100	213
Petroleum	100	275	100	122
Sugar consumption	100	197	100	144
Cotton consumption	100	193	100	155
Tobacco	100	119	100	147

B Concentration in Russian Industry 1901–14

1901

Size of plant	Enterprises	%	Workers	%
Under 100 workers	15,168	83.9	414,785	24.4
101–500 workers	2,288	12.6	492,095	28.9
501–1,000 workers	403	2.2	269,133	15.8
Over 1,000 workers	243	1.3	525,637	30.9
Total	18,102	100	1,701,650	100

1914

Size of plant	Enterprises	%	Workers	%
Under 100 workers	11,117	78.4	348,876	17.8
101–500 workers	2,253	16.1	504,440	25.7
501–1,000 workers	432	3.1	296,347	15.1
Over 1,000 workers	344	2.4	811,197	41.4
Total	14,146	100	1,960,860	100

C Distribution of Employment

Groups	Number of Persons (thousands)			Index (1860=100)	
	1860	1913	1917	1913	1917
Industrial workers	1,660	6,100	7,143	367.4	430.3
Building	350	1,500	1,500	428.6	428.6
Transport	511	1,315	1,857	257.3	363.4
Agricultural wage-earners	700	4,500	5,000	642.8	714.3
Other wage-earners	800	4,065	4,465	508.1	558.1

D Strikes in Petrograd in 1914

Month	Political Strikes			Economic Strikes		
	No. of strikes	No. of strikers	No. of working days lost through strikes	No. of strikes	No. of strikers	No. of working days lost through strikes
July 1–18	–	160,099	–	–	580	–
July 19	26	27,400	48,540	16	10,942	76,914
August	–	–	–	–	–	–
September	1	1,400	280	3	905	1,180
October	–	–	–	2	160	42
November	2	3,150	1,260	3	785	785
December	–	–	–	2	1,020	1,240

E Working and Living Conditions in Petrograd

Petrograd was by far the largest city in the Empire; between 1897 and 1914 its population had grown from 1.26 million to 2.21 million . . . This growth was largely due to the immigration of peasants from the countryside. Every year thousands of peasants flocked to the city in search of work – some to stay for a short while, others to settle permanently. In 1910, no fewer than 68 per cent of the population had been born outside the city . . .

Class divisions were more visible than in Western European cities, where suburbanisation and residential segregation had long been under way. This must have been a factor promoting class consciousness among the workers of St. Petersburg.

The appalling statistics on mortality bear stark testimony to the reality of class division in the city . . . Living conditions in the proletarian districts were sordid and filthy. In 1920 42 per cent of homes were without a water supply or sewage system . . . only a quarter of workers could afford to rent a flat of one or two rooms, and those who could, usually sub-let a part of it. About 70 per cent of single workers and 40 per cent of workers with families lived in shared rooms . . .

The proportion of women in the factory labour force rose from 20.8 per cent in 1900, to 25.7 per cent in 1913, to 33.3 per cent in 1917 . . .

Prior to the war, the employment of children was less widespread in the capital than in Russian industry generally. In 1914 about 8 per cent of the workforce under the Factory Inspectorate in St. Petersburg consisted of youths aged 15 to 17 . . . The labour force in Russia was remarkable for the low proportion of middle-aged workers and the almost complete absence of elderly workers in its ranks . . .

The 1897 census revealed that only 21 per cent of the total population of European Russia was literate . . . In St. Petersburg the rate of literacy was the highest in the country. As early as 1900, 70 per cent of the population aged six or over was literate . . . Working class literacy was higher than the average for the population as a whole . . . A majority of workers in Petrograd in 1917 had had some kind of schooling . . .

Employers paid little heed to standards of safety and hygiene and provided few facilities for their workforces . . . Petrograd had the highest industrial accident rate of any region in Russia . . . At the Putilov works, up to September 1914, there was an average of 15 accidents per month . . . Insurance provision for workers who were injured at work, or who fell sick, was grossly inadequate . . . As late as 1914 Russian workers still worked significantly longer hours than their Western-European counterparts . . .

From S. Smith *Red Petrograd* (1983)

F Russian Agriculture

The basic reason for the low level of the average standard of living in Tsarist Russia was the low productivity of her agriculture, which constituted the livelihood of four fifths of her population . . . The average area of cultivated land per head of the agricultural population worked out at a figure of only about 3 acres, compared with about 13 acres in the USA, 8 acres in Denmark and 4 acres in France and Germany . . . the average yield per acre of arable land in European Russia was . . . scarcely more than a quarter of the yield per acre in the United Kingdom, one third that of eastern Germany and half that of France . . . the yield was also maintained at a low level by the primitive character of farming technique. The three-field system predominated in most parts of the country, which necessitated one third of the arable area lying fallow every year . . .

To these factors in low productivity was added the chronic deficiency of capital among all peasants except a thin upper stratum . . .

All averages about peasant conditions and peasant cultivation are, however, apt to be misleading since they conceal the extensive social differentiation among the peasantry themselves . . . a richer 10 per cent of peasant households . . . owned some 35 per cent of all land . . . An important result was an increasing tendency for the poorer peasantry to seek additional earnings, either by working for wages or by undertaking domestic handicraft industry.

From M. Dobb *Soviet Economic Development Since 1917* (6th ed. 1966)

(N.B. All statistics are based upon Russian sources)

Questions

1 Use Source A, B and C to estimate the extent to which Russia had undergone an industrial revolution in the two decades before the First World War. **(6 marks)**

2 What are the advantages and problems to an historian of using statistics of the type in Sources, A, B, C and D? **(8 marks)**

3 Using your own knowledge, account for the variation of statistics within Source D. **(4 marks)**

4 How useful are Sources D and E to an historian investigating the social, economic and political situation of Russia in 1914? **(6 marks)**

5 What other sources of information, apart from those given above, would an historian seek in order to establish an accurate analysis of Russian society in 1914? **(6 marks)**

2 THE IMPACT OF THE FIRST WORLD WAR

The immediate impact on Russia of the declaration of war in 1914 was positive as far as the government was concerned. Old traditions of patriotism and loyalty reasserted themselves and discontent subsided. However, inadequacies in the political, military, administrative and economic systems created a crisis which was eventually to bring about the downfall of tsarism. The Russian armies, large but often badly supplied and poorly led, suffered serious losses and defeats; and although front-line units generally held firm, demoralisation amongst units in the rear was to be a significant factor in the defeat of the autocracy.

Behind the front line, industrial towns expanded in capacity to meet the requirements of war, yet administrative and economic incapacity prevented adequate food supplies from reaching the growing urban population in sufficient quantities. Government attempts to raise revenue by heavier taxation, borrowing and increasing the money supply caused only inflation and a decline in living standards. The result was heightened discontent.

Nicholas II, Commander-in-Chief of the army from 1915, failed to appreciate the gravity of the situation. The activities of the Tsarina and Rasputin in Petrograd, along with the comings and goings of weak, incompetent ministers, further discredited the government. Inside the Duma, which was growing more and more critical of the running of the war, a Progressive Bloc of Octobrists, Kadets and other liberals demanded constitutional reform and political changes. Virtually all sections of society became alienated from the government.

Professional revolutionaries were scarcely in a position to take advantage of the discontent. Indeed, many of them, including Lenin, were in exile. When revolution came to Petrograd in March 1917, it was to be a largely spontaneous affair, growing out of strikes and demonstrations. Most of Russia was taken by surprise.

A Discontent with the Government's Handling of the War
We now see and know that we can no more legislate with this government than we can lead Russia to victory with it. (*Voices from the left: 'true'.*) We tried earlier to prove that it was impossible to use all the country's strength to fight a war against an external enemy if a war was going on inside the country, for popular support is vital in achieving the nation's aims. It now appears that it is useless to give

proof . . . We say to this government, as the declaration of the Progressive Bloc stated: we will fight you, we will fight by all legal means until you go. (*Voices from the left: 'true'.*) . . .

When the Duma declares again and again that the home front must be organised for a successful war and the government continues to insist that to organise the country means to organise a revolution, and consciously chooses chaos and disorganisation − is this stupidity or treason? (*Voices from the left: 'treason'.*) Moreover, when on the basis of this general discontent the government deliberately busies itself with provoking popular outbursts − for the involvement of the police in the spring disturbances in the factories is proven − when provocation is used to incite disturbances, knowing that they could be a reason for shortening the war − is this done consciously or not? . . .

You must understand why we have no other task than to get rid of this government. You ask why we are carrying on this struggle in wartime. It is only in wartime that they are dangerous. They are dangerous to the war, and therefore in time of war, and in the name of the war, in the name of that which has united us, we now fight them. (*Voices from the left: 'bravo'. Applause.*) . . .

We have many different reasons for being discontented with this government. But all these reasons boil down to one general one: the incompetence and evil intentions of the present government. This is Russia's chief evil, and victory over it will be equal to winning an entire campaign. (*Voices from the left: 'true'.*) And therefore in the name of the millions of victims and of their spilled blood, in the name of our responsibility to those people who elected us, we shall fight until we get a responsible government which is in agreement with the three general principles of our programme. Cabinet members must agree unanimously as to the most urgent tasks, they must agree and be prepared to implement the programme of the Duma majority not just in the implementation of the programme, but in all their actions. A cabinet which does not satisfy these conditions does not deserve the confidence of the Duma and should go. (*Voices: 'bravo'; loud and prolonged applause from the left, centre and left wing of the right.*)

Adapted from a speech by Milyukov to the Fourth Duma, 1 November 1916. Milyukov was leader of the Kadets in the Duma.

B Discontent Inside Russia

The mass of the population is at present in a very troubled mood . . . an exceptional heightening of opposition and bitterness of feeling became very obvious amongst wide sections of the population of

Petrograd. There were more and more frequent complaints about the administration and fierce and relentless criticism of government policies . . . Complaints were openly voiced about the venality of the government, the unbelievable burdens of the war, the unbearable conditions of everyday life. Calls from radical and left-wing elements on the need to 'first defeat the Germans here at home, and then deal with the enemy abroad' began to get a more and more sympathetic hearing . . . a situation was created which was highly favourable to any sort of revolutionary propaganda and actions . . . It is difficult to discount the possibility that German secret agents were operating in such a conducive atmosphere . . .

Without doubt, rumours of this type are greatly exaggerated in comparison with the real situation, but all the same, the position is so serious that attention should be paid to it without delay . . . the conviction has been expressed, without exception, that 'we are on the eve of great events' in comparison with which '1905 was but a toy' . . .

Kadet delegates paint no less sorry a picture of food purchase in Russia. In the words of one of them, 'there is absolute ruin everywhere': the peasantry, cowed by requisitions, unhappy with interference in trading deals by provincial governors and the police, has no desire to sell its grain and other stocks, fearing that they will get only the statutory price . . . As a result, prices are rising everywhere, and goods are disappearing . . .

In the words of another delegate, 'the countryside is now passing through the most critical time, for the first time in Russian history demonstrating the antagonism of town and country' . . . The attitude of the countryside to the war has, right from the outset, been extremely unfavourable, for conscription had a much greater effect there than in the towns. Now in the country there is no belief that the war will be successful . . . The atmosphere in the country has become one of sharp opposition not only to the government, but to other classes of the population: workers, civil servants, the clergy, etc . . .

In the words of other Kadets . . . 'across the whole of Russia the same thing is seen: everyone understands that under the old order the Germans cannot be beaten . . . that the nation itself must interfere in the war . . . This movement, which was to begin with purely economic, has become political and in the future could turn into a serious movement with a definite programme.'

From police reports on the situation in Russia, October 1916.

Questions

1 Using your own knowledge, explain the reference to the 'Progressive Bloc' in Source A (Line 8).   **(3 marks)**

2 What evidence does Source A provide about the problems facing the Russian Government in 1916?   **(6 marks)**

3 To what extent does Source B support Milyukov's claims in Source A about the situation in Russia?   **(7 marks)**

4 What are the uses and limitations of both Sources A and B to an historian investigating the background to the Russian Revolution?

(6 marks)

5 Using Sources A and B and your own knowledge, comment on the assertion that 'The March Revolution was largely unexpected.'

(8 marks)

3 THE FEBRUARY/MARCH REVOLUTION

The March Revolution began with demonstrations and strikes in Petrograd. These were caused chiefly by shortages of bread, but they were also protests at living and working conditions generally. The significant factor was that some military units in Petrograd supported the protestors rather than suppressing them. This was the signal for collapse: some members of the Duma met to try to take control of the situation and were soon to form a Provisional Government. The old Petrograd Soviet of 1905 re-emerged. The Tsar, after vainly attempting to reach Petrograd, was finally persuaded that he was powerless and abdicated.

Several interesting questions emerge from this episode. Some historians have seen the events of March as the inevitable consequence of backward Russia's disastrous involvement in a major war; some have argued that tsarism might have survived had there been a monarch stronger than Nicholas II – one who might have seen sense in compromising with the Progressive Bloc, improving the conduct of the war and possibly retaining some unity within the ruling élite. On the other hand, could a regime which for years had set itself against any idea of fundamental political change realistically adapt to the demands of the time?

The traditional Soviet view of these events plays down the role of the politicians, rather viewing the March events as a victory for the organised masses: the bourgeois-democratic stage on the road to socialist revolution. Indeed, the Provisional Government is branded as a bourgeois-landowner clique put in power by counter-revolutionaries.

A The Social Democrats React to the March Revolution
To all citizens of Russia.
  Workers of the world unite!

Citizens! The strongholds of Russian tsarism have fallen . . . The Russian people through its huge efforts, its blood and at the cost of many lives has thrown off the slavery of centuries.

The task of the working class and the revolutionary army is to create a Provisional revolutionary government which will stand at the head of the new-born republican order.

The Provisional revolutionary government must draw up temporary laws to defend the rights and liberties of the people, to confiscate church, landowners', government and crown lands and transfer them to the people, to introduce the eight-hour working day and to summon a Constituent Assembly on the basis of a suffrage which is universal, without regard to sex, nationality or religion, direct, equal and secret . . .

The hydra of reaction can yet raise its head. The task of the people and its revolutionary government is to put down any counter-revolutionary schemes directed against the people . . .

Citizens, soldiers, wives and mothers! All to battle! To open battle with tsardom and its troops!

From the Manifesto of the Central Committee of the Social Democrats, 27 February 1917.

B The Social Revolutionaries React to the March Revolution

As the danger of counter-revolution has not yet disappeared, the task at the present time is to strengthen the political gains of the Revolution. The conference considers that support for the Provisional Government is absolutely necessary, whilst it carries out its declared programme: an amnesty, the granting of individual freedoms, the repeal of estate, religious and national restrictions and preparation for the Constituent Assembly. The conference reserves the right to change its attitude should the Provisional Government not adhere to the implementation of this programme. The conference also recognises that any attempts to undermine the work of the Provisional Government in the fulfilment of its programme must be combatted.

From a resolution of the Conference of the Petrograd Social Revolutionaries (SRs), 2 March 1917.

C The Kadets React to the March Revolution

The old regime has gone. The State Duma has forgotten its party differences, has united in the name of the salvation of our homeland . . .

All citizens should have confidence in this regime and should combine their efforts to allow the government created by the Duma to complete its great task of liberating Russia from the external enemy and establishing peace inside Russia, on the basis of law, equality and freedom . . .

Forget all your party, class, estate and national differences! . . . Each class, estate and nationality should be able to express its opinions and achieve its aims. The most important slogan now is 'Organisation and Unity', organisation and unity for victory over the external enemy, organisation and unity in internal construction.

11

From an Appeal of the Central Committee of the Kadet Party,
3 March 1917.

D The Nobility React to the March Revolution

In these difficult and great days for Russia, all Russians should put aside their disagreements and should unite around the Provisional Government, now the sole legal authority in Russia, dedicated to defend order and the state system and to the successful conclusion of the war . . . Each one of us should direct all our strength and actions to harmonious work with all devoted sons of our homeland.

From a resolution of the Council of the United Nobility,
10 March 1917.

E The Provisional Government Declares its Aims

Citizens!

The Provisional Government has discussed the military position of the Russian state and has decided that it is its duty to the country to tell the people the whole truth directly and openly.

The old regime left the defence of the country in a seriously disorganised state . . . The Provisional Government, with the vigorous and active cooperation of the people, will devote all its strength to remedying these defects which the old regime left behind . . .

The defence – at whatever cost – of our own national honour and the expulsion of the enemy from inside our borders: this is the first urgent and vital task of our troops, defending the freedom of the people . . . the state is in danger, we must strain every muscle to ensure its salvation. Let not the country's response to this be fruitless despair, or loss of heart, but a united effort to create a single national will.

From the Declaration of the Provisional Government on War Aims,
27 March 1917.

Questions

1 Using your own knowledge, explain the references to the Constituent Assembly (Source A, line 13; Source B, line 7). **(3 marks)**

2 Using your own knowledge and Source A, explain the reaction of the Social Democrats to news of the March Revolution. **(4 marks)**

3 Compare and comment upon the attitudes of the Social Democrats,

the Social Revolutionaries, the Kadets and the nobility towards the Provisional Government (Sources A to D). **(9 marks)**

4 Does Source E suggest that the Provisional Government had the same priorities as the political groupings in the other sources? Explain your answer. **(4 marks)**

5 Using only the evidence of Sources A to E, discuss the problems likely to face the Provisional Government upon its formation after the March Revolution. **(10 marks)**

4 THE STRUGGLE FOR POWER
AFTER THE MARCH REVOLUTION

Following the overthrow of the tsarist regime in the March Revolution, a power vacuum existed in Russia. Two organisations emerged in attempts to fill this vacuum. One was the Provisional Government, which included sections of the Progressive Bloc from the politicians of the Duma, or parliament; the other was the Petrograd Soviet, resurrected from the 1905 Revolution, and dominated by the socialist parties. It was a period of somewhat uneasy co-existence between the two institutions; the time of 'Dual Power', further complicated by uncertainties about the attitude of the army and the return of Lenin to Russia from exile in April 1917. Lenin's attitude towards the new government was very different from that of many of his socialist colleagues: from the start he refused to co-operate and called for a second revolution. Soon the peasants were taking the law into their own hands as the Government delayed the implementation of land reforms. The authority of the Provisional Government, eventually led by Alexander Kerensky, was further weakened by continued failures in the war against Germany, and the threat from both the Left and the Right.

A Demands of the Petrograd Soviet

To the garrison of the Petrograd Military District, to all soldiers of the guard, army, artillery and fleet for immediate and exact execution, and to all the workers of Petrograd for their information.

The Soviet of Workers' and Soldiers' Deputies has decreed: Committees are to be elected immediately in all companies, battalions, regiments . . . and in all naval vessels, from the elected representatives of the rank and file of the above-mentioned units . . .

In all political actions, troop units are subordinate to the Soviet of Workers' and Soldiers' Deputies, and to the committees thereof.

The orders of the Military Commission of the State Duma are to be obeyed, *with the exception of those instances in which they contradict the orders and decrees* of the Soviet of Workers' and Soldiers' Deputies.

All types of arms . . . must be put at the disposal of company and battalion committees, and under their control, and are not, in any case, to be issued to officers, even upon demand . . .

When off duty, in their political, civil and private lives, soldiers should enjoy fully and completely the same rights as all citizens.

In particular, standing at attention and compulsory saluting when off duty are abolished.

From a resolution of the Petrograd Soviet of Workers' and Soldiers' Deputies, published in *Izvestiya*, 2 March 1917

B Support for the Provisional Government?
In agreement with the Petrograd Soviet of Workers' and Soldiers' Deputies, the Provisional Government . . . published a declaration containing a programme of governmental work.

The All-Russian Conference of the Soviets of Workers' and Soldiers' Deputies recognises that this programme includes the basic political demands of Russian democracy . . . the Conference recognises the necessity of gradually gaining political control and influence over the Provisional Government and its local organs so as to persuade it to conduct the most energetic struggle against counter-revolutionary forces . . . and to make preparations for universal peace . . .

The Conference appeals to democracy to support the Provisional Government without assuming responsibility for all the work of the government, as long as the government steadfastly confirms and expands the gains of the revolution and so long as its foreign policy is based on the renunciation of ambitions of territorial expansion . . .

From a resolution by the All-Russian Conference of Soviets, 5 April 1917

C Lenin Demands Action
1. . . . In our attitude towards the war not the slightest concession must be made to 'revolutionary defensism', for even under the new government . . . the war on Russia's part unquestionably remains a predatory imperialist war owing to the capitalist nature of that government . . . the widespread propaganda of this view among the army on active service must be organised.

2. The specific feature of the present situation in Russia is that it represents a *transition* from the first stage of revolution . . . which led to the assumption of power by the bourgeoisie – to *the second stage*, which must place power in the hands of the proletariat and the poor strata of the peasantry . . .

3. No support must be given to the Provisional Government; the utter falsity of its promises must be exposed . . .

4. . . . It must be explained to the masses that the Soviet of Workers' Deputies is the *only possible* form of revolutionary government and that therefore our task is . . . to present a patient, systematic and persistent *explanation* of its errors and tactics . . .

5. . . . Abolition of the police, the army and the bureaucracy . . .
6. . . . Confiscation of all landed estates.
Nationalisation of *all* lands in the country . . .

From Lenin's 'April Theses', 4 April 1917

D A Contemporary View of Lenin

Hardly off the train, he [Lenin] asked the party comrades, 'Why didn't you seize power?' And at once he comes out with his April Theses. . . . He is called mad, delirious . . . The experienced militants censure him; *Pravda* disavows him. But suddenly it becomes apparent that he has the ear of the man in the street, and of the man in the factory and barracks! His whole genius consists only in his ability to say what these people want to say, but do not know how to say . . .

In three weeks, without a struggle, he had a majority in the party; it was no longer a question of fusing with reformists and attempting to stabilise the parliamentary republic . . . But force and courage were required to ensure its success; it was necessary to break with theoretical inertia, and to break with powerful interests.

From V. Serge: *From Lenin To Stalin* (1937).

E A Modern Soviet View of Lenin

The Bolshevik party was waging a determined struggle to win over the masses. The struggle was headed by Lenin who led and guided the Party's Central Committee, the editorial board of the Party's newspaper *Pravda*, and who maintained close contacts with the Party organisations in the provinces . . . He frequently addressed mass rallies and meetings. Lenin's appearance on the platform invariably triggered off the acclamations and enthusiasm of the audience. Lenin's speeches, noted for their profound content and brilliant delivery, inspired the workers and soldiers to a determined struggle. The Bolshevik Party's membership began to grow rapidly.

From Y. Kukushkin: History of the USSR (1981).

Questions

1 Using Source A and your own knowledge, explain why the declaration made in Source A would have appeared threatening to the Provisional Government. **(5 marks)**

2 Using your own knowledge, explain the circumstances in which Lenin issued the April Theses. **(3 marks)**

3 With reference to Source C, summarise Lenin's policy for the
Bolshevik Party.   **(5 marks)**

4 Comment on the differences in Lenin's reception on his return to
Russia, as described in Sources D and E.   **(6 marks)**

5 What questions would an historian ask in order to assess the
reliability of Source D?   **(3 marks)**

6 Using only the evidence of Sources A–E, examine the truth of the
assertion that 'The Provisional Government was doomed to failure
from the beginning of its existence'.   **(8 marks)**

(See page 92 for a specimen source question answer.)

5 THE OCTOBER/NOVEMBER REVOLUTION

The October/November Revolution was undoubtedly a planned *coup d'état*, in the sense that it was organised by a small group of people – the leadership of the Bolshevik party, aided by the Petrograd garrison and Baltic fleet – and it was deliberately designed to overthrow the existing Provisional Government. However, various issues lurk behind these bald facts.

Firstly, it must be emphasised that the Bolsheviks themselves were not unanimous: some of Lenin's colleagues disputed that the time or conditions were ripe for such a *coup* and there were reasons to doubt the likelihood of success of such a venture. Incidents such as the July Days and the Kornilov Revolt, which had demonstrated the weakness of the government, had not been planned or organised by the Bolsheviks, although they exploited the consequences. There is also the moot issue of the Provisional Government itself: had it pursued a different policy, for example towards the continuation of the war, might it have survived? Would the Bolshevik *coup* have succeeded but for Trotsky's energetic exploitation of the situation on behalf of the Military Revolutionary Committee of the Soviet, and his determination to present the *coup* as a victory for the Soviet (representing all left-wing parties) and not just the Bolsheviks? Was it the case that, despite the numerical weakness of the Bolsheviks, there was simply no other viable alternative in November – no other political party or institution had the clear determination and political willpower of Lenin? Did the other parties make a fatal mistake by walking out of the Congress (into Trotsky's 'Dustbin of history') and leaving the field open to the Bolsheviks for a dictatorship? Was the October/November Revolution in fact the victory of a conspiratorial party, or, as in Soviet tradition, the victory of the armed uprising of the working people of Russia?

A Lenin Calls for a Second Revolution

The Bolsheviks, having obtained a majority in the Soviets of Workers' and Soldiers' Deputies of both capitals, can and *must* take state power into their own hands.

They can do so because the active majority of revolutionary elements in the two chief cities is large enough to carry the people with it, to overcome our opponents' resistance to smash them, and to gain and retain power. For the Bolsheviks, by immediately proposing a democratic peace, by immediately giving the land to the peasants and by re-establishing the democratic institutions and liberties which have been distorted and shattered by Kerensky, will form a government which *nobody* will be able to overthrow.

The majority of the people are *on our side*. . . . A Bolshevik government *alone* will satisfy the peasants' demands.

Why must the Bolsheviks assume power *at this very moment*? Because the imminent surrender of Petrograd will reduce our chances a hundred times.

And it is *not in our power* to prevent the surrender of Petrograd while the army is headed by Kerensky and Co. Nor can we 'wait' for the Constituent Assembly, for by surrendering Petrograd Kerensky and Co. *can* always obstruct its convocation. Our Party alone, by seizing power, can secure the Constituent Assembly's convocation . . .

It would be naive to wait until the Bolsheviks achieve a 'formal' majority. No revolution ever waits for *that* . . . History will not forgive us if we do not assume power now.

There is no apparatus? There is an apparatus – the Soviets and the democratic organisations. The international situation *right* now, on *the eve* of the conclusion of a separate peace between the British and the Germans, is *in our favour* . . .

By seizing power both in Moscow and in Petrograd *at once* . . . we shall win *absolutely and unquestionably*.

> From a letter by Lenin to the Central Committee and the Petrograd and Moscow Committees of the Social Democratic Party (SDP).

B Bolshevik Opposition to a Second Revolution

. . . We are most profoundly convinced that to declare at once an armed uprising would mean to stake not only the fate of our party, but also the fate of the Russian and the international revolution. There is no doubt that there are historical situations in which an oppressed class has to acknowledge that it is better to join battle and lose than to surrender without a fight. Is the Russian working class in such a position now? *No, and a thousand times no* . . .

It is said that: (i) the majority of the people in Russia are already for us and (ii) the majority of the international proletariat are for us. Alas! Neither one nor the other is true . . . A majority of workers and a significant part of the army in Russia are for us. But all the rest are in question . . .

And now we come to the second assertion, that supposedly, the majority of the international proletariat are already on our side. This, unfortunately, is not true . . . if we now lose the battle, having staked everything, we will inflict a cruel blow also to the international proletarian revolution . . .

The strength of the proletarian party, of course, is very considerable, but the decisive question is, is the mood among the workers and soldiers of the capital really such, that they themselves see salvation already only in street-fighting and are bursting to go on to the streets? No. This mood does not exist . . .

From a report to the Central Committee of the SDP by Kamenev and Zinoviev, 11 October 1917.

C Trotsky's Version of Events

In October 1917, the working class masses, or at least their leading section, had already come to the firm conviction – on the basis of the experience of the April demonstration, the July days, and the Kornilov events – that neither isolated elemental protests nor reconnoitring operations were any longer on the agenda – but a decisive insurrection for the seizure of power . . .

It is quite clear that to prepare the insurrection and to carry it out under cover of preparing for the Second Soviet Congress and under the slogan of defending it, was of inestimable advantage to us . . . the outcome of the insurrection of October 25 was at least three-quarters settled, if not more, the moment that we opposed the transfer of the Petrograd garrison [to the Front]; created the Revolutionary Military Committee (October 16); appointed our own commissars in all army divisions and institutions; and thereby completely isolated not only the general staff of the Petrograd zone, but also the government . . . The moment that the regiments, upon the instructions of the Revolutionary Military Committee, refused to depart from the city, we had a victorious insurrection in the capital . . . The insurrection of October 25 was only supplementary in character. This is precisely why it was painless . . . Our reference to this insurrection as 'legal' is in the sense that it was an outgrowth of the 'normal' conditions of dual power . . . When we Bolsheviks assumed power in the Petrograd Soviet, we only continued and deepened the methods of dual power . . .

We did not lull the masses with any soviet constitutional illusions, for under the slogan of a struggle for the Second Soviet Congress we won over to our side the bayonets of the revolutionary army and consolidated our gains organisationally . . .

The bourgeoisie derived their succession to power from the state Duma. The conciliationists derived their succession from the soviets; and so did we. But the conciliationists sought to reduce the soviets to nothing; while we were striving to transfer power to the soviets.

From L. Trotsky: *The Lessons of October* (1924)

Questions

1 Using Source A and your own knowledge, explain the reasons for Lenin's call for a second revolution. **(4 marks)**

2 Compare Sources A and B in their arguments on the desirability of immediate revolution and explain the differences. **(8 marks)**

3 Using your own knowledge, explain the references to the July Days and the Kornilov events mentioned in Source C. **(6 marks)**

4 Is Source C closer to Source A or B in its interpretation of the situation in October 1917? **(4 marks)**

5 Using your own knowledge, assess the accuracy of Trotsky's account of the Revolution in Source C. **(4 marks)**

6 Consider any one of Sources A–C and indicate how you would set about assessing its utility to an historian and the reliability of your choice. **(8 marks)**

6 CIVIL WAR

The new Bolshevik government faced many problems in 1917. It had
no blueprint for establishing a new socialist society, it lacked command
of the experts and the traditional machinery of power, and the country
was in a state of war-weariness and disintegration. The Bolsheviks
lacked influence outside a few cities, and they proved to be in a minority
when the elections for the promised Constituent Assembly were held.

Fortunately perhaps for the Bolsheviks, their various opponents were
even weaker and more disorganised. Yet for three years the Bolshevik
government faced a struggle for survival: against the German Army –
a struggle only ended by the costly Treaty of Brest-Litovsk; against
the Whites or various other enemies, both Left and Right, who sought
to overthrow the Bolsheviks; and against foreign interventionists,
seeking first to get Russia back into the war and then to overthrow a
government they detested and feared.

It is sometimes fashionable to depict the struggle of Trotsky's
beleaguered Red Army, fighting several enemies on several fronts, as
an amazing victory by the underdog. It certainly was an achievement.
But there is also evidence to suggest that the Reds had more factors
working in their favour than is commonly recognised, and that
conversely their opponents faced difficult obstacles. More interesting
perhaps is to speculate on the impact of the Civil War on subsequent
Communist attitudes and policies. What effect did their struggle
against the outside world have upon their isolationist mentality? What
effect did the war have upon economic policies and attitudes towards
dissent inside Russia? Can the origins of one-party dictatorship be
traced back to the emergency situation of the Civil War period? Were
wartime attitudes ever in fact discarded?

A Lenin on the Formation of the Red Army

The old army was an instrument of class oppression of the working
people by the bourgeoisie. With the transition of power to the
working and exploited classes there has arisen the need for a new
army as the mainstay of Soviet power at present and the basis for
replacing the regular army by the arming of the whole people in the
near future, and as a support for the coming socialist revolution in
Europe . . .

The Council of People's Commissars resolves to organise a new army, to be called the Workers' and Peasants' Red Army, on the following principles:

(i) The Workers' and Peasants' Red Army is built up from the most conscious and organised elements of the working people.

(ii) Access to its ranks is open to all citizens of the Russian Republic who have attained the age of 18. Every one who is prepared to devote his forces, his life to the defence of the gains of the October Revolution, the power of the Soviets, and socialism can join the Red Army.

From Lenin's decree, 28 January 1918.

B Compulsory Military Training

. . . The Russian Soviet Republic, surrounded on all sides by enemies, has to create its own powerful army to defend the country, while engaged in remaking its social system along Communist lines.

The Workers' and Peasants' Government of the Republic deems it its immediate task to enlist all citizens in universal labour conscription and military service. This work is meeting with stubborn resistance on the part of the bourgeoisie, which refuses to part with its economic privileges and is trying, through conspiracies, uprisings and traitorous deals with foreign imperialists, to regain state power.

To arm the bourgeoisie would mean generating constant strife within the army, thereby paralysing its strength in the fight against the external enemies . . . The Workers' and Peasants' Government will find ways of making the bourgeoisie share, in some form or other, the burden of defending the Republic . . . But in the immediate transitional period military training and arms will be given only to workers and to peasants who do not exploit the labour of others . . .

Female citizens are trained, with their consent, on an equal footing with males . . .

Military training is compulsory for workers . . . and peasants who do not exploit the labour of others . . .

Persons who avoid compulsory training or neglect their duties stemming therefrom shall be called to account.

From a decree by Sverdlov, Chairman of the Central Executive
Committee, 22 April 1918.

C Problems in the Red Army

Krasnov and the foreign capitalists which stand behind his back, have thrown on to the Voronezh front hundreds of hired agents who have penetrated, under various guises, Red Army units and are carrying on their base work, corrupting and inciting men to desert . . .

I declare that from now on an end must be put to this by using merciless means . . .

(i) Every scoundrel who incites anyone to retreat, to desert, or not to fulfil a military order, will be shot.

(ii) Every soldier of the Red Army who voluntarily deserts his military post, will be shot . . .

Death to self-seekers and to traitors!

Death to deserters and to the agents of Krasnov!

Long live the honest soldiers of the Workers' Red Army!

> From Trotsky's order to Red Army troops on the southern front, 24 November 1918.

D A Soviet Historian on the Civil War

The governments of the countries forming the different rival imperialist groupings were at one in their common hatred of the victorious socialist revolution in Russia . . .

The White Guards and foreign interventionists restored a bourgeois-landowner system of government in the areas they overran. Industrial enterprises were handed back to private owners, and the land was taken away from the peasants and given back to the landowners . . . Soviet power lost many vital economic areas, which produced 90 per cent of all the grain, 90 per cent of all the coal, 85 per cent of the iron ore, and 75 per cent of all the pig iron and steel . . . Hundreds of thousands of workers and peasants who were utterly devoted to the cause of the revolution were put to death in numerous prisons and torture chambers . . .

The Communist Party sent the best of its members to join the Red Army . . . By the end of 1918 the Red Army was over 1,700,000 strong. It was a formidable force. Even so, on every battlefront Red Army units had to fight against an enemy who was better equipped, better trained and numerically superior.

> From Y. Kukushkin: *History of the USSR* (1981)

E Another Historian's View of the War

Even Kolchak and Denikin faced, from the winter of 1918–19, a struggle against great odds. The Bolsheviks had had a year to consolidate their position, they controlled most of the military resources of old Russia, they had more popular support, and their forces outnumbered those of the Whites by ten to one.

> From E. Mawdsley: *The Russian Civil War* (1987)

Questions

1 What information can be gleaned from Sources A–C about the problems facing the new Soviet government in 1918?   **(6 marks)**

2 What, according to Sources A and B, were to be the particular characteristics of the new defence forces?   **(4 marks)**

3 Using Source C and your own knowledge, evaluate Trotsky's role as the 'Organiser of Victory' during the Civil War.   **(8 marks)**

4 Compare Sources D and E in their interpretation of the balance of power during the Civil War.   **(6 marks)**

5 What difficulties face any historian attempting to construct an objective account of the Civil War?   **(6 marks)**

7 SOCIALISM OR CAPITALISM 1917–24?

The three years following the October/November Revolution are often characterised as the period of War Communism. Lenin and his colleagues were committed to the unique experiment of transforming capitalism into socialism with no precedent to guide them. Not surprisingly there were disagreements amongst the Bolsheviks themselves as to which was the best course to follow, whilst many workers had their own ideas on grass-roots socialism and were unwilling to submit to bureaucratic controls. In fact, for several months after the Revolution, Lenin was content to let much of the existing industrial system continue, albeit under state supervision – a period sometimes referred to as 'state capitalism'. But with the onset of Civil War the state intervened more directly, with extensive nationalisation, direction of labour and other controls. In the countryside, peasants, although owners of their land, were obliged to submit to grain requisitioning.

The results of this policy of War Communism were disastrous. They included inflation, a decline in industrial and agricultural production, and famine – all with associated political unrest.

War Communism has been a subject of controversy: would the economy have fared better but for the dislocation of war? Controversy was also rife at the time. Some, like Lenin, saw War Communism as a temporary emergency measure forced upon the government. However, radical or 'left-wing' Communists such as Bukharin and Preobrazensky welcomed measures like nationalisation and their results – for example, the collapse of the rouble – as proof of the ideological purity of the government and evidence that the market economy had had its day.

Economic disasters and political threats to the regime, notably the Tambov and Kronstadt Revolts, persuaded Lenin to introduce the New Economic Policy in 1921. Although the 'commanding heights of the economy' remained in state hands, small producers and private traders were allowed to operate again, and the peasants were appeased by the abandonment of requisitioning in favour of a tax in kind and later a money tax. Again, the NEP aroused controversy at the time and since. Was it a hindrance to the development of socialism? Did it herald the return of capitalism? Opponents pointed to the rise of the kulaks (rich peasants) and Nepmen (capitalist speculators and middlemen). Certainly the economic results were impressive, at least in the short term. Interestingly, economic concessions were combined with a tightening, not a relaxation, of discipline in the political sphere.

A Criticisms of the Government's Economic Policies

The productive forces of the country are declining every day. Industry has now become a state pensioner. Most factories and works exist on treasury grants. Labour productivity is alarmingly low, the production of goods is dropping, and the printing of money is increasing rapidly. All this makes the task of the trade unions very difficult. The economic organisations of the working class have to bear the burden of running industry and introducing order into the present economic chaos. However, the economic organisations of the working class are under attack from the Soviet government.

The Soviet government claims that it alone represents the interests of the working class and that, therefore, all other organisations can exist only if they support, without complaint, the internal and external policies of the Council of People's Commissars. Since the October Revolution we have seen endless examples of how big, small or even pigmy commissars have employed every kind of oppression, including bayonets, in their dealings with stubborn proletarian organisations . . .

New trade unions which support the Soviet government have been set up to counteract the opposition of certain trade unions. The government then decides which union really represents the interests of the working class. Besides the persecution of implacable trade unions, other trade unions are being forced into submission and are being transformed into instruments of Soviet power. A scheme for putting the different branches of national industry under the management of trade unions is being worked out. This will lead to greater confusion and to the disintegration of the political life of the country.

From the journal *New Life*, 30 April 1918.

B War Communism in Practice

(i) *Instructions for Requisitioning Grain*

Every food requisition detachment is to consist of not less than 75 men and two or three machine guns.

A commander is to head each detachment. He is to be appointed by the chief commissar responsible for the organisation of food armies. A political commissar is to be appointed by the Commissariat of Food.

The commander is to control purely military and economic activities. The political commissar's duties are (a) to organise local committees of the rural poor and (b) to ensure that the detachment carries out its duties and is full of revolutionary enthusiasm and discipline.

From a decree issued 20 August 1918.

(ii) Every day the post brings information concerning the concealment of grain and other foodstuffs, and the difficulties encountered by the registration commissions in their work in the villages. All this shows the want of consciousness among the masses, who do not realise what chaos such tactics introduce into the general life of the country . . . Everyone is provided for. And yet there is concealment, concealment everywhere, in the hopes of selling grain to town speculators at fabulous prices.

From 'Village Commune', October 1919.

C Debates on War Communism
Was War Communism a response to the war emergency and to collapse, or did it represent an all-out attempt to leap into socialism? . . . It meant different things to different Bolsheviks . . . Some felt that the days of 1918–20 were not only heroic and glorious days of struggle, leading to victory against heavy odds, but were also stages towards socialism and even the gateway to full communism. Some of these men were deeply shocked by the retreat, which seemed to them a betrayal of the revolution. Others saw the necessity of the retreat, but were above all concerned with limiting its consequences and resuming the advance at the earliest date. Still others – some of the future right-wing among them – looked forward to a prolonged pause, and saw in War Communism at best an unavoidable series of excesses . . . Lenin himself admitted that he had been over-sanguine about the War Communism period. More strikingly still, Bukharin swung from the extreme left to become in the end the ideologist of caution and compromise . . .

From A. Nove: *An Economic History of the USSR* (1969).

D A Soviet Justification of NEP
The New Economic Policy (NEP) produced its first positive results in the spring of 1921. The anti-Soviet revolts ceased. The working people were now able to join in the country-wide effort to restore the national economy . . . There were initial signs of recovery in industry . . . The New Economic Policy strengthened the alliance between the workers and peasants and secured the victory of the socialist elements over the capitalist ones. And yet to this day many bourgeois historians continue to portray the New Economic Policy as a departure of the Communist Party and Soviet power from the 'direct road leading to communism' . . .

It was Lenin who began a theoretical struggle against these unscientific inventions . . . Even when he was gravely ill in late 1922 and early 1923, Lenin dictated a series of major works, elaborating ways and means of resolving the problems involved in socialist industrialisation, collectivisation of agriculture, cultural revolution and the development of the Soviet state. Lenin called particular attention to industrial development, notably, of heavy industry . . . Heavy industry was to form the bedrock of socialism . . . Industrialisation created the essential prerequisites for remodelling the country's agriculture along socialist lines. Lenin pointed out that during the transition to socialism in a country with a multiplicity of economic structures, the socialist sector of the national economy should inevitably co-exist for a certain period with the petty-commodity sector, while gradually expanding the sphere of its influence. However, Lenin emphasised that, far from being an evolutionary process, it was a profoundly revolutionary thing with the capitalist elements in the countryside being abolished and the possibility of their revival being effectively ruled out. Lenin saw co-operation in agriculture as the best method of reaching this objective.

From Y. Kukushkin: *History of the USSR* (1981).

E Unease About NEP

In a few years time the NEP restored to Russia an aspect of prosperity. But to many of us this prosperity was sometimes distasteful and often disquieting . . . We had accepted all the necessities of the revolution, including the hardest and most repulsive . . . we had submitted to the bitterest constraint in expectation of the harvest. Then immediately following the Kronstadt killings – our blackest memory – Lenin gave the signal for retreat, saying: 'We must learn from the bourgeoisie. We must learn how to carry on commerce; we shall sell everything except alcohol and icons' . . . and now the cities we ruled over assumed a foreign aspect; we felt ourselves sinking into the mire-paralysed, corrupted . . . Money lubricated and befouled the entire machine just as under capitalism . . . There was gambling, drunkenness, and all the old filth of former times . . . Classes were reborn under our very eyes; at the bottom of the scale, the unemployed receiving 24 roubles a month; at the top, the engineer receiving 800; and between the two, the party functionary with 222 but obtaining a good many things free of charge. There was a growing chasm between the prosperity of the few and the misery of the many . . . Our socialist militia arrested the poor apple-woman who neglected to take out a license, while the fat shopkeeper, enriched by the sale at speculative prices of articles manufactured by our socialist industry, looked on and decided that by and large, order was returning . . . The old militants, those who had experience of prison and the love of ideas, were only a handful; and these few were placed in jobs isolating them from the rank and file . . . We sensed the coming omnipotence of the functionaries.

From V. Serge: *From Lenin To Stalin* (1937).

F Economic Realities

	1913	1920	1921	1922	1923	1924	1925	1926
Factory Production (million roubles)	10251	1401	2004	2619	4005	4660	7739	11083
Coal (million tons)	29	8.7	8.9	9.5	13.7	16.1	18.1	27.6
Electricity (million Kwhs)	1945	–	520	775	1146	1562	2925	3508
Pig iron (thousand tons)	4216	–	116	188	309	755	1535	2441
Steel (thousand tons)	4231	–	183	392	709	1140	2135	3141
Sown area (million ha.)	1.500	–	90.3	77.7	91.7	98.1	104.3	110.3
Grain harvest (million tons)	80.1	46.1	37.6	50.3	56.6	51.4	72.5	76.8

Compiled from various Soviet sources.

Questions

1 What information can be gleaned from Sources A and B about popular reactions to War Communism? **(5 marks)**

2 Using your own knowledge, explain the reference to anti-Soviet revolts in Source D (line 2). **(3 marks)**

3 Compare Sources C, D and E in their interpretations of the motives for, and results of, NEP. **(7 marks)**

4 What are the uses and limitations of Source F as evidence of Soviet economic performance under War Communism and NEP? **(6 marks)**

5 Using only the evidence of Sources A–F, analyse the problems facing Lenin in the construction of a socialist economy between 1918 and 1924. **(9 marks)**

8 POST-REVOLUTIONARY ART AND PROPAGANDA

The Bolshevik Revolution was not just a political and social revolution. It also initiated a cultural explosion. Ardent Communists regarded culture as a force which would inculcate and reflect new social and political attitudes. Although Lenin did not believe that a specifically 'proletarian' culture could be imposed from above overnight, most Communists believed that culture should be enlisted in the service of building socialism.

Most artists welcomed the Revolution as a liberating force. Although many of them were not Communists themselves, they were, like many of their western counterparts, dissatisfied with the values of contemporary society. Artists like Malevich, Tatlin and Mayakovsky claimed to have anticipated the political revolution by their own work. Russian artists had been influenced by Impressionism, Post-Impressionism, Cubism, and their own artistic traditions, but now felt free to experiment even further.

Artists were influential figures after the Revolution. They designed buildings and public spectacles, and sat on government committees. Although there were disagreements within the artistic community – between, for example, Constructivists who believed that art should be applied to functional objects and propaganda, and Suprematists who regarded art as a medium for expressing pure feeling – it was generally a time of experimentation and excitement until Stalin's cultural clampdown at the end of the 1920s.

Cartoons and posters were particularly important in propaganda. In the examples which follow, notice how certain themes recur: enemies of the regime are usually portrayed in a stereotyped way: capitalists, drunkards, kulaks or rich peasants, foreign imperialists, lying journalists, and political opponents such as Mensheviks and Social Revolutionaries usually appear as gross, threatening, evil or angry individuals, in contrast to the determined and sturdy proletarian heroes. Sometimes it is necessary to understand the caption or know some details about the background of the events portrayed, but if the propaganda is to be effective, the message should be clear from the visual source.

Propaganda was a key weapon in the government's armoury after 1917. Propaganda was not regarded as an insidious or underhand weapon of indoctrination, but as a positive force by which certain social and political values could be transmitted to the population and influence its behaviour and entire world-view. The success of the Revolution could be secured through propaganda. The message was spread through literature, posters, film, the theatre, propaganda ships and trains. The effects of this campaign on a population which was still largely illiterate but which was increasingly being educated in the 1920s are still being evaluated.

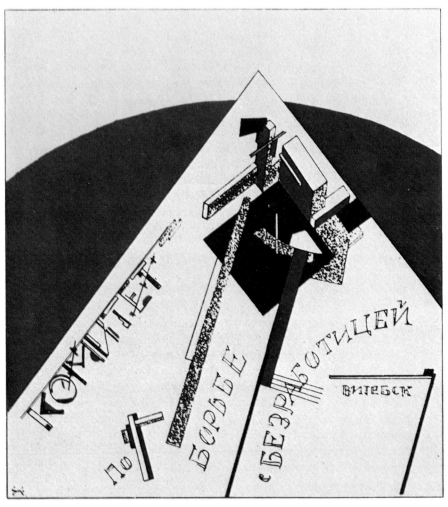

A **Cover design for the book** *The Committee for Fighting Unemployment* **by Lazar Lissitsky, 1919.**

B 'He who is illiterate is like a blind man. Failure and misfortune lie in wait for him on all sides.' Poster by Alexei Radakov, 1920.

C 'If you want something – join up.' Poster by Vladimir Mayakovsky, 1921.
   a) 'Do you want to overcome cold?'
   b) 'Do you want to overcome hunger?'
   c) 'Do you want to eat?'
   d) 'Do you want to drink?'

D 'Setting to work, keep your rifle at hand.' Poster by Vladimir
Lebedev, 1921.

E 'V. Ulyanov (Lenin). 1870–1924.' Poster by Adolf Strakhov, 1924.

F 'The Constituent Assembly.' 1919 poster.

G 'Capital.' 1919 poster.

H 'Kulak blood-sucker.' 1919 poster.

I 'Either death to capitalism or death under the heel of capitalism.'
1919 poster.

J 'Intermediaries of capitalism.' 1926 poster.

K 'In the Grave of Counter-Revolution.' 1920 poster. The references are to Kolchak, Kornilov, Udenich and other White Generals.

41

L 'Appearance of the Holy Spirit to the Apostles.' From the 1920s magazine *Atheist*.

M Drawing from the 1920s magazine *Atheist*.

N 'French fashions in Moscow and Soviet fashions in Paris.' 1924.

Questions

1 Using Sources A–E and your own knowledge, explain the developments in Soviet art between the 1917 Revolution and the late 1920s. **(10 marks)**

2 Identify the main themes of the posters and cartoons shown in Sources F–N. What clues do they give us about the preoccupations of the new Soviet regime? **(10 marks)**

3 Use Sources F–N to comment upon the methods used by Soviet propagandists during this period to get their message across.

(10 marks)

4 How useful are Sources A–N to an historian of Soviet Russia during this period? Explain your answer with reference to individual sources. **(10 marks)**

5 Use your own knowledge to explain how accurately Soviet propaganda reflected conditions inside the USSR during this period, and attempt an evaluation of the effectiveness of propaganda during the 1920s. **(10 marks)**

9 THE DEVELOPMENT OF THE COMMUNIST PARTY

Contrary to the impression sometimes given, the Bolshevik or Communist Party was not a homogeneous organisation under Lenin. In 1917 many SDP committees were jointly Bolshevik and Menshevik in make-up. After 1917 there were threats to the official line from trade unionists in the 'Workers' Opposition' and from left-wing 'Democratic Centralists' – Party members who wanted power to be retained by local soviets rather than by the Party centre.

The 1921 Party Congress was crucial in clamping down on 'factionalism' and internal disagreements. Structural developments ensured that power would lie with the centre. Local Party functionaries and soviets had to accept hierarchical discipline. The Politburo took major policy decisions. The Orgburo carried out executive tasks. The Secretariat effectively controlled all Party appointments and the Party machine. Stalin, a member of the Central Committee, the Orgburo and Politburo, as well as being Secretary of the Party, was effectively able to build up a strong basis of Party support – unlike some of his rivals, notably Trotsky. The problem of 'bureaucratisation' was recognised but not effectively tackled. The key features of political life by 1923 were strict Party discipline and Party control over all key appointments and state institutions.

Party membership underwent several developments. A period of virtually open-door recruitment after the Revolution was later reversed. Further expansion was undertaken, mainly of young Stalinist recruits, under the 'Lenin Enrolment' launched in 1924. Although the bulk of the recruits came from the working class, Party membership increasingly singled out participants as being 'separate' and privileged. However, the Party's position in the countryside remained weak.

Steady recruitment continued under Stalin from 1928, partly due to the requirements of the Five Year Plan, although purges of membership also took place from 1928 onwards.

A Lenin on Party Unity
All class-conscious workers must clearly realise that factionalism of any kind is harmful and cannot be permitted, for no matter how members of individual groups may desire to safeguard party unity, factionalism in practice inevitably leads to the weakening of teamwork and to intensified and repeated attempts by the enemies

of the governing party, who have wormed their way into it, to widen the cleavage and to use it for counter-revolutionary purposes.

The way the enemies of the proletariat take advantage of every deviation from a thoroughly consistent Communist line was perhaps most strikingly shown in the case of the Kronstadt mutiny, when the bourgeois counter-revolutionaries and White Guards in all countries of the world immediately expressed their readiness to accept the slogans of the Soviet system, if only they might thereby secure the overthrow of the dictatorship of the proletariat in Russia . . . These facts fully prove that the White Guards strive, and are able, to disguise themselves as Communists, and even as the most left-wing Communists, solely for the purpose of weakening and destroying the bulwark of the proletarian revolution in Russia. Menshevik leaflets distributed in Petrograd on the eve of the Kronstadt mutiny likewise show how the Mensheviks took advantage of the disagreements and certain rudiments of factionalism in the Russian Communist Party, actually in order to egg on and support the Kronstadt mutineers, the Social Revolutionaries and the White Guards . . .

From Lenin's draft for the Tenth Party Congress, held 8–16 March 1921.

B Problems of Party Unity

Congress draws the attention of all members of the Party to the fact that the unity and cohesion of its ranks . . . is especially necessary at the present time when a number of circumstances are intensifying the hesitancy of the petty bourgeois population of the country . . .

Propaganda about the question must consist, on the one hand, of a detailed explanation of the harmfulness and danger of factionalism . . . and, on the other hand, of an explanation of the uniqueness of the latest tactical moves of the enemies of Soviet power . . .

It is essential that every Party organisation must take the greatest care to ensure that the undoubtedly essential criticism of the shortcomings of the Party . . . is directed not towards the discussion of groups, adhering to some platform or other, etc. but towards the discussion of all Party members . . . Anyone making criticisms must take into account the position of the Party surrounded by enemies and also must strive to correct the mistakes of the Party by active personal participation in soviet and Party work . . .

All Party members must take note that . . . the Party will tirelessly continue testing new methods, will fight bureaucratism with every weapon, will fight for the development of democracy and of initiative,

and for the discovery, unmasking and expulsion of Party hangers on
etc.

Congress orders the immediate dispersal of all groups, without
exception, which were based on some platform or other, and
instructs all organisations to take the greatest care not to permit any
factional speeches. Failure to execute this resolution of the Congress
must result in the unconditional and immediate expulsion from the
Party . . .

From a Resolution by the Tenth Congress of the Communist Party,
8–16 March 1921.

Questions

1 What did Lenin mean by 'factionalism' in Source A (line 1)?

(3 marks)

2 Using Source A and your own knowledge, explain Lenin's concern
to establish a 'consistent Communist line' (line 9). **(6 marks)**

3 What problems are identified by the leadership in Source B, and
what solutions are proposed? **(7 marks)**

10 THE STRUGGLE FOR POWER AFTER LENIN

The problem of the succession troubled Lenin increasingly during the last two years of his life. He had already disagreed with Stalin on several issues, but notably that of the treatment of Georgian nationalism. In Lenin's famous *Testament* he criticised Stalin and Trotsky as potential successors, but offered no positive alternatives.

Even before Lenin's death an unofficial 'triumvirate' of Zinoviev, Kamenev and Stalin existed with the purpose of blocking Trotsky. Trostky was widely mistrusted for his background and personality, and contributed to his political demise by his own tactical mistakes. Stalin skilfully established his claim to be Lenin's heir after the latter's death in 1924, whilst his rivals argued among themselves. Arguments over economic policy – particularly attitudes towards the peasantry and the best method of industrialisation – and personal differences determined a series of alliances. Trotsky, Zinoviev and Kamenev formed the 'United Opposition' in 1926, a marriage of pure convenience, to challenge the Bukharin pro-peasant line; but they themselves were defeated and expelled from the Party. In 1928 the 'Right Opposition' of Bukharin, Rykov and Tomsky was formed to oppose rapid industrialisation; but it was defeated by Stalin and his largely compliant Party.

It is important to understand the succession struggle not purely in terms of personalities: there were genuine ideological differences also, chiefly concerning the best path to industrialisation. The role of Stalin is also interesting. It is fashionable to decry his skills, and many contemporaries underestimated him. Yet he skilfully played the role of moderate in the middle, outmanoeuvred rivals and played on their weaknesses, and built up a very effective power base.

Part One

A Lenin Worries About the Succession

Comrade Stalin, having become General Secretary, has concentrated an enormous power in his hands; and I am not sure that he always knows how to use that power with sufficient caution. On the other hand, Comrade Trotsky . . . is distinguished not only by his exceptional abilities – personally he is, to be sure, the most able man in the present Central Committee – but also by his too far-reaching self-confidence and a disposition to be too much attracted by the purely administrative side of affairs.

These two qualities of the two most able leaders of the present Central Committees might, quite innocently, lead to a split; if our Party does not take measures to prevent it, a split might arise unexpectedly. I will not characterise the other members of the Central Committee as to their personal qualities. I will only remind you that the October episode of Zinoviev and Kamenev was not, of course, accidental but that it ought as little to be used against them personally as the non-Bolshevism of Trotsky . . .

Bukharin is not only the most valuable and biggest theoretician of the Party, but may legitimately be considered the favourite of the whole Party; but his theoretical views can only with the very greatest doubt be regarded as fully Marxist . . .

From Lenin's *Testament*, 4 January 1923.

B Trotsky on Stalin

Lenin undoubtedly valued highly certain of Stalin's traits: his firmness of character, tenacity, stubbornness, even ruthlessness, and craftiness – qualities necessary in war and consequently in its general staff. But Lenin was far from thinking that these gifts, even on an extraordinary scale, were sufficient for the leadership of the Party and the state. Lenin saw in Stalin a revolutionist, but not a statesman in the grand style. Theory had too high an importance for Lenin in a political struggle. Nobody considered Stalin a theoretician, and he himself up to 1924 never made any pretence to this vocation. On the contrary, his weak theoretical grounding was too well known in a small circle. Stalin is not acquainted with the West . . . He was never brought into the discussion of problems of the international workers' movement. And finally Stalin was not – this is less important, but not without significance – either a writer or an orator in the strict sense of the word. His articles, in spite of all the author's caution, are loaded not only with theoretical blunders and naiveties, but also with crude sins against the Russian language. In the eyes of Lenin, Stalin's value was wholly in the sphere of Party administration and machine manoeuvring. But even here Lenin had substantial reservations . . . Stalin meanwhile was more and more broadly and indiscriminately using the possibilities of the revolutionary dictatorship for the recruiting of people personally obligated and devoted to him. In his position as General Secretary he became the dispenser of favour and fortune . . .

From L. Trotsky: 'On the Suppressed Testament of Lenin',
31 December 1932.

C Stalin at Lenin's Funeral

In leaving us, Comrade Lenin commanded us to hold high and pure the great calling of Party Member. We swear to thee, Comrade Lenin, to honour thy command. In leaving us, Comrade Lenin commanded us to keep the unity of our Party as the apple of our eye. We swear to thee, Comrade Lenin, to honour thy command. In leaving us, Comrade Lenin ordered us to maintain and strengthen the dictatorship of the proletariat. We swear to thee, Comrade Lenin, to exert our full strength in honouring thy command. In leaving us, Comrade Lenin ordered us to strengthen with all our might the union of workers and peasants. We swear to thee, Comrade Lenin, to honour thy command. In leaving us, Comrade Lenin ordered us to strengthen and expand the Union of the Republics. We swear to thee, Comrade Lenin, to honour thy command. In leaving us, Comrade Lenin enjoined us to be faithful to the Communist International. We swear to thee, Comrade Lenin, that we shall dedicate our lives to the enlargement and reinforcement of the union of the workers of the whole world, the Communist International.

Stalin's speech at the funeral of Lenin, January 1924.

D Stalin on the Way Ahead

Comrades, we Communists are people of a special mould . . . We are those who form the army of the great proletarian strategist, the army of Comrade Lenin. There is nothing higher than the honour of belonging to this army . . . It is not given to everyone to be a member of such a party . . . It is the sons of the working class, the sons of want and struggle . . . who before all should be members of such a party . . .

From Stalin's speech to the Congress of Soviets, 26 January 1924.

E Condemnation of Trotsky

. . . The opposition, headed by Trotsky, came forth with the slogan of smashing the Party apparatus, and tried to shift the centre of gravity of the struggle against bureaucratism in the governmental apparatus to 'bureaucratism' in the apparatus of the Party . . .

Trotsky came out with vague insinuations about the degeneration of the basic cadres of our Party and thereby tried to undermine the authority of the Central Committee, which between congresses is the only representative of the whole Party. Trotsky . . . permitted accusations which could not but evoke unrest in broad circles of the working class and a stormy protest in the ranks of our Party . . .

The opposition clearly violated the decision of the Tenth Congress of the Russian Communist Party which prohibited the formation of factions within the Party. The opposition has replaced the Bolshevik view of the Party as a monolithic whole with the view of the Party as the sum of all possible tendencies and factions. These tendencies, factions and groupings, according to the 'new' view of the opposition, must have equal rights in the Party . . . Such a view of the Party has nothing in common with Leninism. The factional work of the opposition cannot but become a threat to the unity of the state apparatus. The factional moves of the opposition have enlivened the hopes of all enemies of the Party, including the west-European bourgeoisie, for a split in the ranks of the Russian Communist Party . . .

The All-Union Party Conference comes to the conclusion that in the person of the present opposition we have before us not only an attempt at the revision of Bolshevism, not only a departure from Leninism, but also a clearly expressed *petty-bourgeois deviation* . . .

In the situation where the Russian Communist Party, embodying the dictatorship of the proletariat, enjoys a monopoly of legality in the country, it is unavoidable that the least stable groups of Communists should sometimes give in to non-proletarian influences. The Party as a whole must see these dangers and watchfully guard the proletarian line of the Party.

A systematic and energetic struggle of our whole Party against this petty-bourgeois deviation is essential . . .

> From a resolution of the Thirteenth Conference of the Russian Communist Party 'On the Results of the Controversy and on the Petty-Bourgeois Deviation in the Party', January 1924.

Questions

1 Using your own knowledge, explain the references in Source A to:

   a) 'The October episode of Zinoviev and Kamenev' (lines 13–14).

   (2 marks)

   b) Distrust of Bukharin's 'theoretical views' (line 19).   **(2 marks)**

2 Do Sources C and D confirm Trotsky's evaluation of Stalin's abilities and character in source B?   **(8 marks)**

3 a) What criticisms of Trotsky are made in Source E?   **(4 marks)**

   b) What are the uses and limitations of Source E to an historian?

   (5 marks)

4 Using the evidence of Sources A–E and your own knowledge, explain Stalin's defeat of Trotsky in the struggle for the succession to Lenin.

   (9 marks)

Part Two

A Stalin's Tactics in the 1920s

[From 1923] Stalin demonstrated a consummate ability at intrigue and the manipulation of the Party controls . . .

Stalin intimates that he played the part of peacemaker; that he was opposed to expulsions; opposed to 'the letting of blood' – thus permitting all the unpopularity of his campaigns to fall on Zinoviev. He likewise manoeuvres so as to make Zinoviev and Kamenev appear responsible for all the failures of the agrarian policy which led to the enrichment of a minority of peasants and a critical shortage in the state grain collections. He lets Zinoviev take the responsibility for the defeats of the International . . .

. . . Stalin completes the job of packing all the Party secretariats (excepting those of the Leningrad region, controlled by Zinoviev) with his creatures. In 1926 his work is done; he is master of the Party, of a Party in whose ranks utter silence reigns, a Party in which majorities, docile because they profit by being docile, do nothing but vote the resolutions prescribed by the Central Committee and submitted by the secretaries. At the Fourteenth Congress, Zinoviev is suddenly put in the minority, isolated, and rendered responsible for all internal and foreign difficulties . . . The controversy turns on questions of prime importance. Stalin announces the new policy of 'socialism in one country,' which would be totally meaningless if it did not signify a renunciation of international solidarity. No compromise is possible. Stalin enters into combination with the rightists of the Central Committee [Rykov, Tomsky, Bukharin] to continue an agrarian policy of enriching the kulaks. Stalin completes his task of strangling the Party: Zinoviev goes over to the opposition; in an embarrassing *volte face* he joins his adversary of the day before, Trotsky, accepting his programme for democratisation of the party – and consequently of the government – for industrialisation and pressure on the 'kulak, the nepmen, and the bureaucrat'.

From V. Serge: *From Lenin to Stalin* (1937).

B Stalin on the Expulsion of the Left Opposition

How could it happen that the entire Party, as a whole, and following it the working class too, so thoroughly isolated the opposition? After all, the opposition are headed by well-known people with well-known names, people who know how to advertise themselves (*voices: 'Quite right!'*), people who are not afflicted with modesty (*applause*) and are able to blow their own trumpets.

It happened because the leading groups of the opposition proved to be a group of petty-bourgeois intellectuals divorced from life, divorced from the revolution, divorced from the Party, from the working class. (*Voices: 'Quite right!' Applause*) . . .

Have we the dictatorship of the proletariat or not? Rather a strange question. (*Laughter.*) Nevertheless, the opposition raise it in every one of their statements. The opposition say that we are in a state of Thermidor degeneration [A reference to the overthrow of Robespierre and the Jacobins in the French Revolution]. What does that mean? It means that we do not have the dictatorship of the proletariat, that our economics and our politics are a failure, are going backwards, that we are not going towards socialism, but towards capitalism. This, of course, is strange and foolish. But the opposition insist on it . . .

You will ask: how could such an opposition come into being among us; where are their social roots? I think that the social roots of the opposition lie in the fact that the urban petty-bourgeois strata are being ruined under the conditions of our development, in the fact that these strata are discontented with the regime of the dictatorship of the proletariat, in the striving of these strata to change this regime, to 'improve' it in the spirit of establishing bourgeois democracy . . .

Why did the Party expel Trotsky and Zinoviev? Because they are the *organisers* of the entire anti-Party opposition *(voices: 'Quite right!')*, because they set themselves the aim of breaking the laws of the Party, because they thought that nobody would dare to touch them, because they wanted to create for themselves the privileged position of nobles in the Party . . .

If the opposition want to be in the Party let them submit to the will of the Party, to its laws, to its instructions, without reservations. Without equivocation. If they refuse to do that, let them go wherever they please. (*Voices: 'Quite right!' Applause*). We do not want new laws providing privileges for the opposition, and we will not create them. (*Applause*).

The question is raised about terms. We have only one set of terms: the opposition must disarm wholly and entirely, in ideological and organisational respects. (*Voices: 'Quite right!' Prolonged applause*).

They must renounce their anti-Bolshevik views openly and honestly, before the whole world. (*Voices: 'Quite right!' Prolonged applause*) . . .

> From Stalin's 'Political Report of the Central Committee to the Fifteenth Congress of the CPSU' 3 December 1927.

C Stalin Against the Right

What is the theoretical basis for the blindness and bewilderment of Bukharin's group? I think that the theoretical basis for this blindness and bewilderment is Bukharin's incorrect, non-Marxian approach to the question of the class struggle in our country. I have in mind Bukharin's non-Marxist theory that the kulaks will grow into socialism – his failure to understand the mechanism of the class struggle under the dictatorship of the proletariat . . .

What can there be in common between Bukharin's theory that the kulaks will grow into socialism and Lenin's theory of the dictatorship as a fierce class struggle? Obviously, there is not, nor can there be, anything in common between them. Bukharin thinks that under the dictatorship of the proletariat the class struggle must *subside* and *pass away* so that the abolition of classes may be brought about. Lenin, on the contrary, teaches us that classes can be abolished only by means of a stubborn class struggle, which under the dictatorship of the proletariat becomes *even fiercer* than it was before the dictatorship of the proletariat . . .

Discontent with the Leninist policy of the Party in its leadership of the peasantry, discontent with our grain-purchasing policy, with our policy of developing collective and state farms to the utmost, and lastly, the desire to 'unfetter' the market and to establish complete freedom of private trade – there you have the underlying reason for Bukharin's screams about military-feudal exploitation of the peasantry . . .

We have two different plans of economic policy.

The Party's Plan . . . *the key to the reconstruction of agriculture is the speedy rate of development of our industry.*

Bukharin's Plan . . . *The key to the reconstruction of agriculture is the development of individual peasant farming.*

That is how it works out, comrades. Bukharin's plan is a plan to *reduce* the rate of development of industry and to *undermine* the new forms of the [worker-peasant] bond. Such are our divergencies . . .

. . . The fight against the Right deviation is one of the most decisive duties of our Party. If we, in our own ranks, in our own Party, in the political General Staff of the proletariat, which is directing the movement and is leading the proletariat forward – if we in this General Staff should tolerate the free existence and the free functioning of the Right deviationists, who are trying to demobilise the Party, to demoralise the working class, to adapt our policy to the tastes of the 'Soviet' bourgeoisie, and thus yield to the difficulties of our socialist construction – if we should tolerate all this, what would it mean? Would it not mean that we want to send the revolution downhill, demoralise our socialist construction, flee from difficulties, surrender our positions to the capitalist elements?

Does Bukharin's group understand that to refuse to fight the Right deviation is to betray the working class, to betray the revolution? Does Bukharin's group understand that unless we overcome the Right deviation and the conciliationist tendency, it will be impossible to overcome the difficulties facing us . . . it will be impossible to achieve decisive successes in socialist construction? . . .

The Party demands that they [the Bukharinites] should wage a determined struggle against the Right deviation and the conciliationist tendency, side by side with all the members of the Central Committee of our party . . . Either the Bukharinites will fulfil this demand of the Party, in which case the Party will welcome them, or they will not, in which case they will have only themselves to blame . . .

From Stalin's Speech 'The Right Deviation in the CPSU' to the Central Committee, April 1929.

Questions

1 Using your own knowledge and Source A, explain why controversy about 'socialism in one country' (line 21) was important in the 1920s.
(5 marks)

2 According to Source A, how did Stalin achieve his aims during the 1920s? **(4 marks)**

3 Assess Stalin's tactics and political skills demonstrated in Sources B and C. **(8 marks)**

4 Using your own knowledge and Source C, explain the reasoning behind Stalin's agricultural policy. **(5 marks)**

5 Do Sources A–C show that Stalin was motivated more by personal considerations than ideological considerations? **(8 marks)**

11 ECONOMIC
TRANSFORMATION 1928–41

By the late 1920s Stalin was in a position to implement a policy of rapid industrial growth, with a largely unified and disciplined Party at his command. The goal was to make the USSR a first-ranking industrial and military power. This modernisation had to be paid for by extracting the bulk of the resources from the peasantry, who still made up 80 per cent of the population.

The Procurements Crisis of 1928 proved that grain supplies were still uncertain. Stalin's solution was to resurrect the methods of War Communism, that is, forced requisitioning. However, it was now to be accompanied by an all-out drive to collectivisation, which, it was hoped, would increase the efficiency of farming, destroy the 'capitalist' elements in the countryside (the kulaks), and increase the Party's hold over the countryside. Despite resistance, collectivisation was essentially complete by 1936.

There is controversy over the results. Certainly collectivisation was a human disaster for many peasants. Several million peasants died; grain and meat production fell drastically until the late 1930s. Yet, from the government's point of view, the proportion of agricultural production at its disposal increased, and the Party now controlled the countryside.

The decision to engage in long-term planning for industrialisation was taken in 1927. Since detailed information or theoretical understanding was lacking, the targets set were arbitrary. The results of the three Five-Year Plans between 1928 and 1941 are a subject of controversy and statistics vary, but undoubtedly there were successes in certain key areas, and Russia's international position in comparative terms improved. Alongside this, agricultural output remained static and living conditions actually declined. In effect, Stalin succeeded in building socialism in one country by increasing the fiscal burden on all sections of society and relying on various incentives – but also, ultimately, force. Whether the industrialisation successes could have been achieved by less dictatorial means is open to debate.

Part One

A The Reasons for Collectivisation

... the decision to undertake overall collectivisation had its roots in the grain crisis at the beginning of 1928. Stalin's ideas on policy germinated during the testing time of this crisis, though only in essentials, for *at that stage he was concerned only with a short-term policy of moderate aims*, but by reason of the growing crisis he was constantly obliged to extend the objectives with which he had set out at the beginning of the year ...

During his visit to Siberia, where he had gone to urge and compel the party officials to take the grain ruthlessly ... he became aware of the urgent necessity for establishing strongpoints in the countryside, similar to those the regime had built up in the towns ... It is at this point also that he expressed the thought that the Soviet regime was 'walking on two unequal legs' – the socialist sector in the towns and the private sector in the villages – and that this could not go on indefinitely. It can be deduced from this ... that he no longer believed in NEP as a viable policy ... As he saw it, matters must be so arranged that the state would be absolutely sure of having at its disposal some 250 million poods of grain (in other words, about a third of the quantity required by the end of the Five-Year Plan) ...

Stalin knew, and told the Central Committee in a speech which was secret at the time, that the peasants would have to pay a tribute for the requirements of industrialisation. This was Preobrazhensky's theory, but with none of the latter's scruples or reservations.

From M. Lewin: *The Immediate Background of Soviet Collectivization* (1965).

B Stalin Encounters Problems

... by 20 February 1930, we had *over-fulfilled* the Five-Year Plan of collectivisation by more than 100 per cent ...

But successes have their seamy side ... People not infrequently become intoxicated by such successes; they become dizzy with success, lose all sense of proportion and the capacity to understand realities ... Collective farms must not be established by force. That would be foolish and reactionary. The collective-farm movement must rest on the active support of the main mass of the peasantry ...

We know that in a number of areas of Turkestan there have already been attempts to 'overtake and outstrip' the advanced areas of the USSR by threatening to use armed force, by threatening that peasants who are not yet ready to join the collective farms will be deprived of irrigation water and manufactured goods ...

How could there have arisen in our midst such block-headed exercises in 'socialisation', such ludicrous attempts to overleap oneself?

From an article by Stalin in *Pravda*, 2 March 1930.

C The Peasants Give Their Views on Collectivisation
The members of the *kolkhoz* have for two months received no pay for their labour, which consists of transporting wood and feed. Of the revenue, 50 per cent goes to the *kolkhoz* treasury, 50 per cent for taxes and rent. What remains for the workers? No one knows . . . All this lends credence to the kulaks' assertion that a 'new serfdom' is being instituted . . . The *kolkhozes* are emptying. Eighty peasants in this hole-in-the-ground came to the public prosecutor to complain that they had been forced by violence to join the *kolkhoz* . . . The peasants have replied to the forced collectivisation by selling their possessions, sabotaging the work and revolting . . . The peasants' assemblies are being purged. A nearby soviet has just announced the expulsion of 20 poor peasants, some of whom are sincerely devoted to the regime. All are condemned as 'agents of the kulaks.' Their crime is that they have not always kept silent, that they have said their condition has grown worse, and asked if there would be another Five-Year Plan.

From letters quoted in V. Serge: *From Lenin To Stalin* (1937).

D A Soviet Version of the Problems
The kulaks were resisting the collective farm movement in a bid to retain their positions, cost what it might . . . The kulaks and their hirelings began to wage a campaign of terror against those who supported and worked for collectivisation . . .

In late 1927 and early 1928, the kulaks everywhere began to refuse to sell their produce at state-fixed prices. They hid grain and sabotaged the grain trade in a bid to destabilise the socialist economy, thereby threatening the very existence of Soviet power . . . The kulaks launched a campaign of anti-collective-farm propaganda, sabotage and wrecking . . .

The increasingly acute class struggle in the countryside made the liquidation of the kulaks as a class a top-priority task . . .

In 1937, the country had 6,000 operational machine-and-tractor stations . . . However, much of agriculture's demand for machinery remained unsatisfied. Many collective farms had as yet failed to exploit the advantages of collective farming to the full. Only some of the collective farms had succeeded in obtaining high crop-yields and stable harvests. The animal husbandry sector continued to lag behind.

From Y. Kukushkin: *History of the USSR* (1981).

E Statistics on Collectivisation

	1928	1929	1930	1931	1932	1933	1934	1935
Grain harvest (million tons)	73.3	71.7	83.5	69.5	69.6	68.4	67.6	75
Cattle (million head)	70.5	67.1	52.5	47.9	40.7	38.4	42.4	49.3
Pigs (million head)	26	20.4	13.6	14.4	11.6	12.1	17.4	22.6
Sheep/goats (m head)	146.7	147	108.8	77.7	52.1	50.2	51.9	61.1

From Soviet sources.

Questions

1 Explain the reference to 'Preobrazhensky's theory' (Source A lines 22–3). **(3 marks)**

2 Using your own knowledge and Source A, explain Stalin's motives for abandoning the NEP. **(6 marks)**

3 Examine the view that Source B tells us more about Stalin's political skills than the reality of collectivisation. **(4 marks)**

4 What questions would you ask of Source C to evaluate its reliability? **(5 marks)**

5 To what extent does Source D support the picture of collectivisation painted in Source C? **(6 marks)**

6 How far does Source E support Source D in its portrayal of the effects of collectivisation? **(6 marks)**

Part Two

A Stalin Justifies the Pace of Industrial Development
It is sometimes asked whether it is not possible to slow down the tempo a bit, to put a check on the movement. No, comrades, it is not possible! The tempo must not be reduced! On the contrary, we must increase it as much as is within our powers and possibilities. This is

dictated to us by our obligations to the workers and peasants of the USSR. This is dictated to us by our obligations to the working class of the whole world.

To slacken the tempo would mean falling behind. And those who fall behind get beaten. But we do not want to be beaten. No, we refuse to be beaten! One feature of the history of old Russia was the continual beatings she suffered for falling behind, for her backwardness . . . for military backwardness, for cultural backwardness, for political backwardness, for industrial backwardness, for agricultural backwardness. She was beaten because to do so was profitable and could be done with impunity . . . It is the jungle law of capitalism. You are backward, you are weak – therefore you are wrong; hence, you can be beaten and enslaved. You are mighty – therefore you are right; hence, we must be wary of you. That is why we must no longer lag behind . . .

Do you want our socialist fatherland to be beaten and to lose its independence? If you do not want this you must put an end to its backwardness in the shortest possible time and develop a genuine Bolshevik tempo in building up its socialist system of economy. There is no other way. That is why Lenin said during the October Revolution: 'Either perish, or overtake and outstrip the advanced capitalist countries.'

We are 50 or 100 years behind the advanced countries. We must make good this distance in ten years. Either we do it, or they crush us.

From an article by Stalin, written in 1931.

B Achievements of the Five-Year Plans

	First Five-Year Plan (1928–32)	Second Five-Year Plan (1933–37)
National Income		
1 Official Soviet estimate (1926–7 prices)	91.5	96.1
2 Western estimates	70.2	66.5
Industrial Production		
1 Official Soviet estimate (1926–7 prices)	100.7	103.0
2 Western estimates	64.9	83.3
3 Official Soviet estimate, producer goods (1926–7 prices)	127.6	121.3
4 Official Soviet estimate, consumer goods (1926–7 prices)	80.5	85.4

Agricultural Production

1	Official Soviet estimates (1926–7 prices)	57.8	62.6–76.9
2	Western estimates	50.9	70.9

Wages

1	Average money wage	143.9	173.6
2	Average real wage, official Soviet estimate	31.9	102.6
3	Average real wage, Western estimate	26	65.8

Labour Productivity, Industry

1	Official Soviet estimate	65.1	–
2	Western estimates	39	–

(NB: Western estimates are an average of researches by various Western economists.)

C A Soviet View of Industrial Achievements

While the economies of the capitalist countries were sinking ever deeper into recession, the Soviet economy was booming. The laying of a firm foundation for a socialist economy created favourable conditions for the further progress of the country's national economy in the Second Five-Year Plan period, 1933–1937. These years saw the commissioning of the industrial projects started during the preceding Five-Year Plan period. The second sections of the Magnitogorsk and Kuznetsk iron and steel complexes were completed ahead of schedule. At the start of the Five-Year Plan a major victory was scored on the industrialisation front when the Urals and Novo-Kramatorsk heavy engineering plants went into operation ... The construction of factories in light industry was substantially expanded ...

Good progress was made in constructing new railways and motorways ... 4,500 new factories, plants, mines and power-stations were commissioned, three times as many as in the First Five-Year period ...

The country's working class continued to grow ... By the mid-1930s, Soviet industry, saturated with up-to-date equipment and machinery, had an adequate army of skilled workers. The material and cultural standard of the workers had risen, as had the level of their political awareness ...

The key economic task of the Second Five-Year Plan period – technical re-equipment of the national economy – was fulfilled ... During the Second Five-Year Plan period, industrial output went up by 120 per cent. The USSR moved into first place in Europe and second in the world in gross industrial output. Whereas during the First Five-Year Plan period the rapid growth of industrial output was largely due to the physical expansion of the scale of industrial production along with the increase in the size of the work force, in the Second Five-Year Plan period it rose thanks to the growing labour productivity.

From Y. Kukushkin: *History of the USSR* (1981).

D Living Conditions

The proper assessment of living standards at this time is rendered almost impossible not only by the existence of rationing, price differences, and shortages, but also of queues, decline in quality, neglect of consumer requirements . . . Therefore any figures comparing wages and prices are bound greatly to understate the decline in living standards . . .

In order to facilitate the mobilisation of the working class for the 'great tasks of building socialism', and so as to avoid any organised protest about living standards or working conditions, the trade unions . . . were instructed to act primarily as organisers and mobilisers in the interests of plan fulfilment . . . The protective role of the unions was greatly reduced . . . The inclusion in the picture of the peasants would certainly make it worse, in particular in the period 1928–34 . . . 1933 was the culmination of the most precipitous peacetime decline in living standards known in recorded history.

From A. Nove: *An Economic History of the USSR* (1969).

Questions

1 To what extent does Source A provide an adequate explanation for both the motives and the methods of Stalin in introducing the Five-Year Plans? **(6 marks)**

2 What are the value and limitations of Source B in an investigation into the achievements of the First and Second Five-Year Plans? **(8 marks)**

3 To what extent do Sources C and D support the evidence of Source B concerning the impact of the Five-Year Plans? **(8 marks)**

4 What other evidence would an historian need for a detailed investigation into the results of the Five-Year Plans? **(8 marks)**

12 THE PURGES

Terror did not begin with Stalin. At the end of 1917 the Cheka had been formed to deal with counter-revolution, and terror was practised on both sides during the Civil War. The secret police (GPU) were active again during the collectivisation drive, and supervised forced labour during the industrialisation drive. In 1934 all aspects of internal state security were co-ordinated in the NKVD. This latter body was given new powers following the murder of Kirov in the same year. The time of the Great Terror began – but now the purges meant not expulsion from the Party, but imprisonment, exile or death, with or without a trial. Between 1936 and 1938 many prominent Bolsheviks, plus millions of smaller fry, suffered in this way.

Stalin's motives are still a matter of debate. He was certainly suspicious of old Bolsheviks, who were more likely to oppose his policies; he wanted to increase his own power base, even beyond the Party; perhaps he wanted to instil general fear and suspicion, a policy of divide and rule. The human costs were enormous, and are now the subject of much agonising, in the USSR as elsewhere. However, it is also important to stress that Stalin's policies won support from a significant section of the younger generation who were able to rise through talent, whatever their backgrounds. This new élite were deliberately raised above the rest of the population in terms of privileges and power – the new Soviet bureaucracy.

The hardening of political attitudes in the later 1930s was accompanied on the one hand by some improvements in wages, education and social services, and on the other hand by an emphasis on greater discipline in the family and increased censorship of cultural activity.

A Bukharin on the Background to the Purges

In 1932, it is true, there were no actual revolts, but . . . half of the country was stricken with famine. The workers were on short rations. The productivity of labour had greatly fallen, and there was no way of raising it . . . The predominant view in Party circles was that Stalin had led the country into an impasse by his policy, that he had roused the peasants against the Party, and that the situation could be saved only by his removal from Party domination. Many influential members of the Central Committee were of this opinion . . .

Kirov played an important part in the Politburo. He was a 100 per cent supporter of the 'general line,' and distinguished himself during its operation by great energy and inflexibility. This caused Stalin to value him highly. But there was always a certain independence in Kirov's attitude which annoyed Stalin. The story is told that Stalin had prevented Kirov from attending the meetings of the Politburo in Moscow for several months under the pretext that his presence in Leningrad was indispensable. However, Stalin could never make up his mind to take strong measures against Kirov . . .

Kirov stood for the idea of *abolition of the terror*, both in general and inside the Party . . . Kirov's line of thought ran as follows . . . as the economic situation continued to improve, the broad masses of the population would become more and more reconciled to the government; the number of 'internal foes' would diminish. It was now the task of the Party to rally those forces which would support it in the new phase of economic development, and thus to broaden the foundation upon which Soviet power was based . . .

Early in the summer of 1933, when it became certain that the harvest would be good, Kamenev, Zinoviev and a number of other former members of the opposition were once again admitted as members of the Party . . . and some of them actually received invitations to the Party Congress [February 1934]. At that congress Kirov appeared in triumph . . . During the recesses there was discussion as to who had had the more tumultuous reception, Kirov or Stalin . . .

[After Kirov's assassination] . . . the trend was in quite the opposite direction: not toward reconciliation inside the Party, but toward intensification of the terror inside the Party to its logical conclusion, to the stage of *physical extermination of all those whose Party past might make them opponents of Stalin or aspirants to his power.* Today, I have not the slightest doubt that it was at that very period, between the murder of Kirov and the second Kamenev Trial, that Stalin made his decision and mapped out his plan of 'reforms' . . . The determining reason for Stalin's decision was his realisation, arrived at on the basis of reports and information reaching him, that *the mood of the majority of the old Party workers was really one of bitterness and hostility toward him* . . . As Stalin perceived it, the reasons for the hostility toward him lay in *the basic psychology of the old Bolsheviks.* Having grown up under the conditions of revolutionary struggle against the old regime, we had all been trained in the psychology of oppositionists, of irreconcilable nonconformists . . .

The conclusion he [Stalin] drew from all this was certainly daring: if the old Bolsheviks, the group constituting today the ruling caste in the country, are unfit to perform this function, it is necessary to remove them from their posts, to create a new ruling caste.

> From Bukharin's talks with the Menshevik historian Boris Nicolaevsky, published in *Letter of an Old Bolshevik* (1938).

B An Insight into Stalin's Psychology?

[Stalin mused] . . . Yes, the history of mankind was the history of class struggle, but the leader emerged as the expression of class, and therefore the history of mankind was the history of its leaders and its rulers. Idealism did not come into it. The spirit of an epoch was determined by the man who made the epoch himself . . .

. . . all opponents, past, present, and future, had to be liquidated and would be liquidated. The sole socialist country in the world could survive only if it were unshakably stable, and this would also be seen as a sign of its stability by the outside world. The state must be strong in case of war; the state must be mighty if it wants peace. It must be feared.

In order to turn a peasant society into an industrialised country, countless material and human sacrifices were necessary. The people must accept this. But it would not be achieved by enthusiasm alone. The people would have to be forced to accept the sacrifices, and for this a powerful authority was needed, an authority that inspired fear . . . the theory of undying class war provided for all such possibilities. If a few million people had to perish in the process, history would forgive Comrade Stalin . . . All the great rulers had been harsh . . . Sending Trotsky into exile out of the country had been a humane act, and therefore it had been a mistaken one: Trotsky was at large and still active. He would not send Zinoviev and Kamenev into exile abroad: they were going to serve as the first foundation stone of the bastion of fear he must build in order to defend the nation and the country. And they would be followed by their allies. Bukharin was one of their allies.

> From A. Rybakov: *Children of the Arbat* (published in Britain in 1988, after suppression in the USSR for 20 years).

C The Reasoning Behind the Terror

The principles and aims of mass terror have nothing in common with ordinary police work or with security. The only purpose of terror is intimidation. To plunge the whole country into a state of chronic fear, the number of victims must be raised to astronomical levels, and on every floor of every building there must always be several apartments from which the tenants have suddenly been taken away. The remaining inhabitants will be model citizens for the rest of their lives . . . The only essential thing for those who rule by terror is not to overlook the new generations growing up without faith in their elders, and to keep on repeating the process in a systematic fashion.

From N. Mandelstam: *Hope Against Hope* (1971).

D Confessions in the Show Trials
(a) Bukharin

I shall now speak of myself, of the reasons for my repentance. Of course, it must be admitted that incriminating evidence plays a very important part. For three months I refused to say anything. Then I began to testify. Why? Because while I was in prison I made a re-evaluation of my entire past. For when you ask yourself: 'If you must die, what are you dying for?' – an absolutely black vacuity [emptiness] suddenly arises before you with startling vividness. There was nothing to die for, if one wanted to die unrepented. And on the contrary, everything positive that glistens in the Soviet Union acquires new dimensions in a man's mind. This in the end disarmed me completely and led me to bend my knees before the Party and the country. And when you ask yourself: 'Very well, suppose you do not die; suppose by some miracle you remain alive, again what for? Isolated from everybody, an enemy of the people, in an inhuman position, completely isolated from everything that constitutes the essence of life . . . ' And at once the same reply arises. And at such moments, Citizens Judges, everything personal. . . . all the rancour, pride, and a number of other things, fall away, disappear, and in addition, when the reverberations of the broad international struggle reach your ear, all this in its entirety does its work, and the result is the complete moral victory of the USSR over its kneeling opponents . . .

The point, of course, is not this repentance . . . The court can pass its verdict without it. The confession of the accused is not essential . . . But here we have also the internal demolition of the forces of counter-revolution. And one must be a Trotsky not to lay down one's arms.

b) Yagoda

I want to correct the Procurator and make an objection on a part of the charges he has made . . . The Procurator is not right in considering me a member of the centre of the bloc . . . I am not a spy and have never been one . . . it is untrue to say that I was an accomplice in the murder of Kirov . . . I have committed heinous crimes. I realise this. It is hard to live after such crimes, it is hard to sit in prisons for tens of years. But it is terrible to die with such a stigma. Even from behind the bars I would like to see the further flourishing of the country which I betrayed . . .

Our laws and our court differ greatly from the laws and the courts of all bourgeois countries . . . this court, when trying a criminal case, does not base itself on laws as on a dogma, but is guided by revolutionary expediency. Our country is mighty, strong as never before, purged of spies, diversionists, terrorists and other scum, and I ask you, Citizens Judges, in passing sentence on me, to consider whether there is revolutionary expediency in my execution now?

> From the 'Report of the Court Proceedings in the Case of the Anti-Soviet "Bloc of Rights and Trotskyites" heard before the Military Collegium of the Supreme Court of the USSR, Moscow', March 2–13 1938.

Questions

1 Using your own knowledge, explain why Stalin was anxious to take action against Zinoviev and Kamenev (Source B line 22). **(5 marks)**

2 Compare Sources A, B and C in their interpretations of the motives for the Purges. **(8 marks)**

3 What issues of reliability are raised by the evidence of Sources A and B? **(5 marks)**

4 Using your own knowledge, explain why *either* Bukharin *or* Yagoda were victims of Stalin's Purges. **(4 marks)**

5 Using only the evidence of Sources A–D, assess the validity of the statement that 'Stalin's Terror achieved the effects that he intended.' **(8 marks)**

13 PROPAGANDA IN THE STALINIST ERA

Cultural freedom, in so far as it had ever existed in the Soviet Union, disappeared with the rise of Stalin. The Communist Party under Stalin made a conscious attempt to control all manifestations of culture and refine existing methods of propaganda to serve the ends of the Party and of the state. The campaigns of collectivisation and industrialisation were accompanied by a vicious propaganda campaign against groups and individuals labelled as enemies of the regime. These ranged from saboteurs supposedly carrying out the orders of the exiled Trotsky, to dispossessed kulaks and reluctant shirkers and slackers in the factories. The rise of Hitler and the Nazi menace brought forth a new wave of anti-fascist propaganda. The USSR under Stalin possessed a siege mentality: the first workers' state was surrounded by external enemies and harboured internal traitors. As the class war intensified, so the people had to be made aware of the need for vigilance, defence, and the ruthless unmasking of all who stood in the way of the path to socialism. These propagandist themes were reinforced by cultural developments such as 'Socialist Realism', with its optimistic images of worker heroes and heroines, true Soviet patriots whose dedication would ensure the victory of socialism whatever their individual fates.

Most totalitarian states and dictatorships employ propaganda as a means of moulding a national consciousness in the direction desired by the regime, and the USSR was no exception. Indeed, some of its propaganda methods were admired and copied elsewhere, including Nazi Germany. Some of the cartoons and posters shown here contain stereotypes similar to those of the immediate post-revolutionary and Civil War period – for example the enemies of the Five-Year Plans. But new concerns also appear in this collection: notably an awareness of the threat posed by the rise of Fascism, particularly in Germany, and the desire for a front against Fascism, as well as propaganda related to the issues of collectivisation and industrialisation.

A 'They try to stop the Revolution' – Mensheviks and SRs. 1920s poster.

B 'The Harvest.' Magazine illustration from the 1920s. The peasant is surrounded by the kulak, the priest and the boot-legger, as he tries to protect his harvest.

C 'International Red Day – Day of the Mobilisation of the World Proletariat against Imperialist War.' 1929 poster.

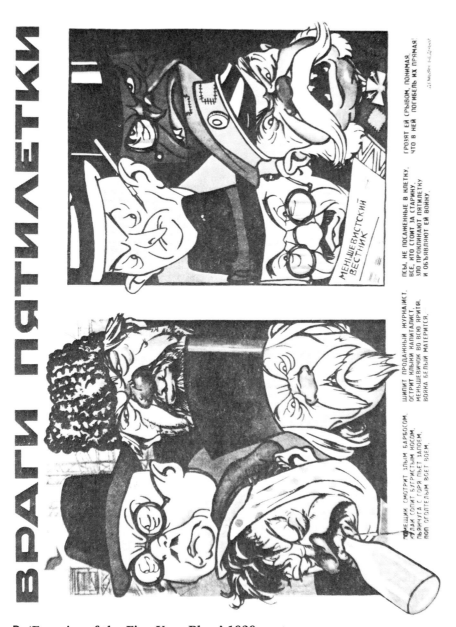

D 'Enemies of the Five-Year Plan.' 1929 poster.

E 'Fascism is on the offensive. We will crush the foul creature with a powerful counter-offensive of the proletariat.' 1930 poster.

„РОТ ФРОНТ!''—рабочий клич всемирно-боевой,
Угроза банде всей банкирско-биржевой.
Биржевикам уже дня не провесть в покое,
        Им все мерещится такое.
На нас им кинуться б,—да боязно: афронт
Возможен, ух какой! Гром грянет—клич ответный:

—„Да здравствует всесветный РОТ ФРОНТ!''
И не спасут тогда банкиров пушки, танки!
        Не выдержат их биржи, банки
        Напора рот-фронтовиков!
И полетят в помойный хлам останки
        Биржевиков!

                        Демьян Бедный

F 'Red Front.' 1932 poster.

G 'The Kingdom of the Church – a Kingdom in Chains.' From the *Anti-Religious Alphabet* of 1932.

H 'In the Cradle of German Fascism – Good Day Adolf Hitler.' 1933.

I 'Karl and Pygmies.' 1933 poster. The pygmies are shouting: 'we repudiate, we forbid, we banish, we revise it, we curse.'

J 'The Five-Year Plan (Completed in Four Years).' 1933 poster.

K 'Seven Problems – One Answer! (The Five-Year Plan in Four Years).'
1930s poster.

Questions

1 Identify which of the propaganda posters (Sources A–K) relate to Stalin's economic policies. **(5 marks)**

2 Identify which of the propaganda posters (Sources A–K) relate to Stalin's concerns outside the USSR. **(5 marks)**

3 Use Sources A–K to explain what methods were used by Soviet propagandists in the Stalinist period to create hatred of opponents and other 'enemies' of the regime. **(10 marks)**

4 Choose any four of Sources A–K and for each explain:
a) the message of the source
b) at whom it was probably aimed
c) how you would evaluate its impact. **(4 x 6 marks)**

5 'All political propaganda is biased and therefore of little value to an historian.' Do you agree? You should refer to the sources in your answer. **(12 marks)**

14 A CULTURAL REVOLUTION?

Initially the Russian Revolution was viewed by Bolsheviks as the start not only of a political and economic transformation of their country, but also of its cultural metamorphosis. Lenin and other Bolsheviks were concerned to raise the general educational and cultural level of the masses and to abolish the notion of a separate cultural élite. However, there was to be a distinct change in emphasis. Experimentation in the arts was encouraged in the early 1920s, and new media such as the radio and film were eagerly exploited, albeit to serve the purposes of socialist society. However, from the late 1920s creative freedom was a thing of the past. Stalin, as part of his struggle with the opposition of the Right, warned the Party against the emergence of a new bourgeoisie and cultural intelligentsia, divorced from the experiences of proletarian life. Communist youth was enrolled in the struggle against bourgeois culture. 'Socialist Realism' became the order of the day: art must serve politics, and more specifically it must be optimistic, relevant to everyday life, heroic, and with a deliberate message. All publications were subject to Party control. Some notable works were produced, but artistic freedom was a concept totally alien to these new principles.

A Lenin on Culture
All educational work in the Soviet Republic of workers and peasants, in the field of political education in general and in the field of art in particular, should be imbued with the spirit of the class struggle being waged by the proletariat for the successful achievement of the aims of its dictatorship, i.e. the overthrow of the bourgeoisie, the abolition of classes, and the elimination of all forms of exploitation of man by man.

From a resolution by Lenin, 8 October 1920.

B 1920s Cultural Policy
. . . As the class war in general has not ended, neither has it ended on the literary front. In a class society there is not, nor can there be a neutral art . . .

It must be remembered, however, that this problem is infinitely more complicated than other problems being solved by the proletariat . . . the proletariat, the class which was culturally deprived, was unable to develop its own literature, its own characteristic artistic forms, its own style. Although the proletariat has ready infallible criteria regarding the socio-political content of any literary work, it does not have such definite answers to all questions of artistic form . . .

While discouraging anti-proletarian and anti-revolutionary elements . . . the Party should have a patient attitude toward intermediate ideological formations, patiently aiding those inevitably numerous formations to develop in the process of ever closer comradely cooperation with the cultural forces of communism . . .

Communist criticism should fight mercilessly against counter-revolutionary phenomena in literature; and yet at the same time show the greatest tact, attention and patience toward all those groups which can and will join the proletariat . . . Marxist criticism should have as its slogan 'to learn,' and should resist every appearance of cheap judgement and ignorant arrogance in its own milieu.

While it has infallible criteria of judgement regarding the class content of literary tendencies, the Party as a whole must not bind itself to any one tendency in the field of literary form . . . the Party cannot support any one faction in literature . . . just as it cannot by resolutions settle questions of the form of the family, though in general it does and should lead in the development of new ways of life . . .

Therefore the Party should declare itself in favour of the free competition of various groups and tendencies in this province. Any other solution of the problem would be an official, bureaucratic pseudo-solution . . . While morally and materially supporting proletarian and proletarian-peasant literature, and aiding the fellow-travellers, the Party cannot offer a monopoly of any of these groups, even the one most proletarian in its ideology. For this would be to destroy proletarian literature itself . . .

> From a resolution of the Central Committee of the Russian Communist Party, 'On the Policy of the Party in the Field of Literature', 1 July 1925.

C Communism and Literature

Our literature is the youngest of all the literatures of all countries and peoples . . . There does not exist and never has existed any literature other than Soviet literature . . . making its basic subject matter the life of the working class and the peasantry and their struggle for socialism . . .

In our country the main heroes of a literary work are the active builders of the new life – men and women workers and collective farmers, engineers, Komsomols, Pioneers . . . Soviet literature must be able to portray our heroes and to see our tomorrow. This will not be utopian since our tomorrow is being prepared by planned and conscious work today.

> From Zhdanov's address to the Soviet Writers' Congress, 1934.
> Zhdanov was an intellectual and leading Communist.

D Socialist Realism

The Communist-Leninist Party . . . have made it the object of their daring, sage and indefatigable activity to free the working masses from the age-old yoke of an old and outworn history, of the capitalist development of culture, which today has glaringly exposed all its vices and its creative decrepitude. And it is from the height of this great aim that we honest writers of the Union of Soviets must examine, appraise and organise our work . . .

As the principal hero of our books we should choose labour . . .

The Party leadership of literature must be thoroughly purged of all philistine influences . . . the Party leadership must, in all its conduct, show a morally authoritative force. This force must imbue literary workers first and foremost with a consciousness of their collective responsibility for all that happens in their midst.

> From M. Gorky: 'Soviet Literature' – a speech at the First All-Union
> Congress of Soviet Writers, August 1934.

E Literature and the Personality Cult

O great Stalin, O leader of the peoples,
Thou who broughtest man to birth.
Thou who fructifiest the earth,
Thou who restorest the centuries,
Thou who makest bloom the spring,
Thou who makest vibrate the musical chords . . .
Thou, splendour of my spring, O Thou,
Sun reflected by millions of hearts . . .

> Poem printed in *Pravda*, 1 February 1935.

F A Western Interpretation of Soviet Culture

There is, it must be candidly admitted, in the USSR of today, little of the sort of culture that used to be recognised as such in the Oxford or Cambridge common rooms, or in the artistic coteries of Bloomsbury or Chelsea; and even less governmental recognition of it, or encouragement to it . . .

Is it unfair to say that the British devotees of culture not only accept as inevitable the exclusion of the masses from the 'realms of gold' in which they themselves find so much virtuous enjoyment, but also secretly rejoice at their own exclusive possession of something in which the common lump of men cannot share . . . ? In the usage of Soviet communism there is, in the conception of culture, no such connotation of inevitable exclusiveness, of a pleasant aloofness, or of a consciousness of superiority. It is, at any rate, definitely the policy of the Soviet Government . . . that the possession of culture shall be made, not necessarily identical or equal, but genuinely universal . . . Soviet Communists actually believe that, by a sustained effort of self-sacrifice on the part of the older people, the entire generation that is growing up in the USSR can be raised to a high level of culture. There will be some who will see in that very belief, and in the strenuous efforts that it inspires, a real evidence of culture in the best sense of the word.

From S. & B. Webb: *Soviet Communism: A New Civilisation* (1935).

Questions

1 a) Compare Sources A, B, C and D in their views on the role of culture in Soviet society. **(8 marks)**
   b) How do you explain any differences? **(3 marks)**

2 Does Source E meet the criteria of Socialist Realism discussed in Sources C and D? **(4 marks)**

3 a) According to Source F, what was the difference between Soviet culture and British culture in the 1930s? **(4 marks)**
   b) How far does the view of Soviet culture in Source F reflect the views of Sources A – D? **(4 marks)**

4 Using your own knowledge of any examples of Soviet culture in the 1920s and 1930s, estimate the extent to which there was a cultural revolution during these years. **(7 marks)**

15 SOVIET JOKES

Political jokes flourish under totalitarian regimes. They serve a useful function as a safety valve, allowing individuals to express to each other their feelings about their rulers, their political systems, and life generally. Sometimes jokes are the only outlet, since such feelings can often not be expressed in the 'official' media. The relaying of political jokes in such regimes can be dangerous, but their popularity is such that they are often told by functionaries of the regimes themselves.

A Lenin dies and finds himself at the Pearly Gates. He asks Saint Peter to let him in.

'You can't come in here,' Saint Peter says, 'You agitated and started a revolution! You're a troublemaker! Go to hell, where you belong!'

Lenin shrugs his shoulders and turns away.

Some time later Saint Peter comes to hell to check on Lucifer and to see if everything is being administered according to the Providential Plan.

'Sorry, I can't talk now,' says Lucifer curtly as he glances at his watch. 'I'm late for a Party rally.'

B A man, sitting in his flat, heard a loud knock at the door.

'Who is it?' he asked anxiously.

'It is the Angel of Death.'

'Phew!' the man exclaimed. 'For a moment I thought it was the secret police!'

C A Party joke from 1932.

Q. What does it mean when there is food in the town but no food in the country?

A. A Left, Trotskyist deviation.

Q. What does it mean when there is food in the country but no food in the town?

A. A Right, Bukharinite deviation.

Q. What does it mean when there is no food in the country and no food in the town?

A. The correct application of the general line.

Q. And what does it mean where there is food both in the country and in the town?

A. The horrors of capitalism.

D Stalin dies and goes to hell.

Some time later, Saint Peter is surprised to see several devils hammering on the Pearly Gates and demanding to be let in.

'What do you want?' asks Saint Peter, suspecting a devious trick.

'We want to get in,' a devil replies.

'Why?'

The devils prostrate themselves before Saint Peter. 'We want political asylum!'

E Stalin wanted to get a true picture of what people thought of him, so he went in disguise into a cinema.

After the main film, a newsreel was shown which naturally highlighted Stalin in every scene. All the audience stood up amidst thunderous, unrelenting applause. Stalin remained modestly seated.

After a few moments the man next to Stalin nudged him and said gently: 'Most people feel the same way as you, comrade. But it would be safer if you stood up.'

F Stalin complained to a colleague in the Kremlin that his office was infested by mice and that nothing, including traps and poison, had succeeded in getting rid of them.

'No problem!' the colleague replied. 'Just declare that your office is a collective farm. Half the mice will run away and the other half will die of starvation!'

G Q. Why do the secret police always travel in threes?

A. One can read, one can write, and the third is there to keep an eye on the two intellectuals.

H A flock of sheep was stopped by frontier guards at the Russo-Finnish border.

'Why do you want to leave Russia?' the guards asked.

''It's the NKVD,' replied the terrified sheep. 'Beria's ordered them to arrest all elephants.'

'But you're not elephants!' the guards exclaimed.

'Yes,' said the sheep. 'But try telling that to the NKVD!'

Questions

1 What do these jokes tell us about popular reactions to:
   a) Lenin   c) life generally in the USSR at this time?
   b) Stalin   d) the secret police   **(16 marks)**

2 Do jokes have any uses for historians of Soviet Russia or of totalitarian regimes generally? You should refer to these sources or use any others you know of in your answer.   **(12 marks)**

16 HISTORIOGRAPHY

Historians' views are influenced by many factors: their own personal prejudices; the climate in which they are writing – but in the case of the Russian Revolution there are added complications. The Russian Revolution still has contemporary relevance and repercussions and therefore it is additionally difficult for historians to be detached, or to see things with perspective. Soviet historians for long accepted the Marxist view that history, like any science, cannot be impartial. Equally, some western historians have been far from impartial in their approach, whatever their expressed intentions. Extreme reactions have sometimes been the response to events such as Stalin's collectivisation programme and the Purges. In the late 1980s there was a radical reappraisal of Soviet history in progress within the USSR itself.

The most fruitful approach for the student is probably to focus on certain issues and consider why historical controversy has arisen. Why have historians arrived at particular conclusions? Some of the key issues have already been touched upon in this book. They include: how far can Lenin be held responsible for the events which followed his death? Was Stalinism inevitable for the USSR to build socialism in a backward country? Was the dictatorship of the Party inevitable, given the circumstances of the Revolution? Were personalities more significant than ideas? Could the USSR have survived war with Germany in 1941 without the economic measures of the previous ten years?

By their nature, these questions cannot be easily answered; but it can be a fruitful and interesting method of research to investigate and compare the approaches of various historians on these topics.

A Problems of a German Historian
Decades later, many of us still feel too close to the Revolution to be able to bridge the gulf between what had been and what was to come: old Russia and new Russia were profoundly dissimilar and still cannot be reconciled . . . The controversies which swirl about the year 1917 have acquired a lengthy history of their own, and monuments are more numerous than eyewitnesses. Nevertheless, time has scarcely tempered the feeling that the Russian Revolution marks a turning point in our century and in ourselves.

There can be no doubt that the October revolutionaries understood their victory as signifying a 'departure from previous history' (A. Weber) . . . The heirs to the Revolution still cling to this conception.

With the October Revolution, it is said, the world entered the era of socialism and communism. No other revolution in world history can compare with such an epochal [remarkable] event . . .

From a historical point of view, however, it is impossible to accept the notion that all links with the past were severed in 1917. There was continuity within change, as well as an awareness of the continuing presence of the old regime . . . After 1930 a Stalin-inspired patriotism, 'Soviet patriotism', began to resurrect old Russia . . . The new society was now expected to draw reinforcement and strength from pride in Russia's glorious past. This past could not not exploited if revolutionary traditions alone were emphasised . . . According to the new teaching, a people is eternal and its culture survives the ages . . .

Despite all that can be said about the advantages and disadvantages of historical perspective, one fact remains clear; widespread unanimity exists regarding many aspects of the Russian Revolution, though opinion concerning its minutiae and ultimate significance may vary.

From D. Geyer (ed.): *The Russian Revolution* (1987)

B An American Historian's View

The highways and byways of contemporary history are strewn with pitfalls and dead-end strets; within this general field there is probably no more dangerous ground than that devoted to the study of the Soviet Union. For here, all the problems and difficulties facing the contemporary historian are bound to come up sooner or later, usually with a vengeance . . .

Most professional historians of Russia failed to understand the significance of 1917 because their outlook had been shaped exclusively by the elements of continuity in Russian history . . . For that reason most of them were quite incapable of recognising and assessing correctly the elements of change . . .

. . . One must be deeply distrustful of those who claim to deal with the Russian Revolution or Soviet history from a standpoint of strict impartiality. On closer inspection either this impartial attitude turns out not to be genuine, or the authors' competence doubtful . . .

. . . If it is to be of any value, a book on the Russian Revolution written now ought to be different in approach from one written by contemporary observers . . . Objectivity does not imply that the later historian has to be a mediator between extreme positions; he may be as extreme in his condemnation or as ardent in his admiration as any contemporary. But he can no longer be public prosecutor or counsel for the defence; he is obliged to look at his subject from a higher vantage point, to take into consideration all factors and possibilities, however inconvenient and unpalatable . . .

If excessive moral indignation may blind the historian, the absence of moral judgement leads him into absurd and indefensible positions . . .

The study of Soviet history . . . has taught us little apart from the ever present need to be wary of sweeping generalisations . . . In Soviet history (as in the history of other countries) there has been no inevitability, but there has been something in the nature of a theory of probability . . . There seems to be freedom of choice at major historical turning points . . . One can talk, therefore, about possibilities and probabilities in Soviet history, which at different times have assumed varying importance; now bordering on the inevitable, now being so vague or conflicting in character as to make the prospect of success or failure a highly hazardous affair . . .

Other questions arise from an occupation with Soviet history: Soviet historians . . . have been severely critical of the schools of thought which have refused to see the decisive role of economic and social history. But what are the driving forces in Soviet history? Can Lenin's and Stalin's policies be explained on this basis?

What then remains in the 1980s of the various approaches propagated only a decade earlier? Little, apart from such commonsense notions that economics and geography matter, that national character is also important and that a study of a Soviet middletown would, no doubt, be quite revealing . . .

Our ideal historian of the Soviet Union . . . will not reveal absolute laws and certainties, but provide a better understanding of probabilities.

From W. Laquer (ed.): *The Fate of the Revolution* (1987).

C A Modern Soviet Historian's View

Several generations of Soviet people have breathed a heavy ideological smog. History has been falsified . . . Virtually every period, event and issue has been misrepresented until relatively recently.

The majority of history books followed suit, with certain events being passed over in silence. Our own Soviet history suffered most . . . Historical consciousness was maimed . . . Historical consciousness also determines the way in which the economy is run. Our fake national history inhibits the development of our economy today.

Take the aggressive attitude of some officials and many private citizens towards those who want to lease land or form a co-operative. Their attitude is dogmatic: black and white. It is their misfortune rather than their guilt, for this kind of mentality has been cultivated for decades in the intellectual world . . .

Stalin's regime was unnatural, illegal, and contradicted the ideas, traditions and history of socialism, it was imposed by force, using mass criminal reprisals. To make it appear legitimate there had to be a fake history . . .

I think it is abnormal that biographies of Kamenev, Zinoviev, Bukharin and others who at one time stood at the helm of the Party and the state were written only by foreign historians . . . I have spoken of what have become known as the blank spots of Soviet history, but have not yet covered the largest blank spot, that of Leon Trotsky . . . Stalin's vision of Trotsky is unacceptable, for it is false throughout. I have no personal sympathy for Trotsky, but I do believe he deserves a truthful analysis. Trotsky, for one thing, played a very positive role in the October Revolution, during the Civil War and the restoration of the economy . . .

It is only historical studies devoid of all sorts of ideological dogmas that are capable of comprehending our past, and restoring our social identity. This has to be a prerequisite of every society.

> From interview with Y. Afanasyev: 'Filling in the Blank Spots in Soviet History' in *History Today*, February 1989.

Questions

1 Study Sources A, B and C and identify the difficulties which face the student of Soviet history. **(10 marks)**

2 Consider any *one* of Sources A, B or C and explain how far you agree or disagree with the interpretation it contains, referring (if you wish) to any example from Soviet history. **(10 marks)**

3 Consider any historian or book on Soviet history with which you are acquainted, and assess your choice in the light of the considerations discussed in these three sources. **(10 marks)**

17 DEALING WITH EXAMINATION QUESTIONS

Specimen Source Question Answer

(See pages 16–17)

1 Using Source A and your own knowledge, explain why the declaration made in Source A would have appeared threatening to the Provisional Government. **(5 marks)**

The order states that, although the Petrograd Soviet promises to respect the State Duma, in certain circumstances it may disobey its decrees if it thinks fit to do so. The Soviet also demands that soldiers' committees, not officers, should control weapons. Likewise implied is a narrowing of differences between soldiers and civilians, and between ranks in the army. All this might be seen as a threat to military discipline – of great importance to a new government whose internal authority might possibly need a reliable buttress, particularly in the light of its desire to continue the war. Failure to maintain the loyalty of the army had cost the Tsar dear, as it was to cost the Provisional Government later in 1917.

2 Using your own knowledge, explain the circumstances in which Lenin issued the April Theses. **(3 marks)**

Lenin issued the Theses upon his arrival in Petrograd from Finland. He was returning from exile, aided by the Germans. At this time the official Bolshevik line was to support the Provisional Government and the changes made by the March Revolution, and therefore Lenin was pursuing a radical new policy.

3 With reference to Source C, summarise Lenin's policy for the Bolshevik Party. **(5 marks)**

Lenin issued various demands: first, that at a time when further revolution was upon the horizon, the Bolsheviks should oppose Russia's continued participation in the war; second, that they should engage in propaganda for the benefit of the proletariat, explaining the errors of bourgeois policies and explaining the next stage of revolution; and third, that they should oppose the Provisional Government. The Theses also outline specific and radical economic, social and political demands – for example, nationalisation of the land.

4 Comment on the differences in Lenin's reception on his return to Russia, as described in Sources D and E. **(6 marks)**

Source D implies that Lenin's message was not immediately welcome; he was criticised and disowned by elements of his own Party, although his message was welcome to the man in the street, which accounted for Lenin's eventual victory. Source E, however, suggests that there was no opposition; the impression is that Lenin immediately carried all before him.

Victor Serge in Source D was closer to the truth: Lenin did meet initial opposition from Bolsheviks who had been in Russia for some time and felt that their policy of conditional co-operation with the Government was correct. Kukushkin's book, a later source by a Soviet historian, is likely to gloss over Lenin's difficulties in the interest of promoting the official line that Lenin was always right and that the momentum towards revolution was unstoppable!

5 What questions would an historian ask in order to assess the reliability of Source D? **(3 marks)**

An historian would ask: who was Serge? What were his political leanings? Is he reliable as a witness? Did he get his information first- or second-hand? Was he present during the events? Were his views, published in 1937, coloured by hindsight?

6 Using only the evidence of Sources A–E, examine the truth of the assertion that 'The Provisional Government was doomed to failure from the beginning of its existence'. **(8 marks)**

Source A implies that the Provisional Government was likely to face difficulties since its authority was only conditionally accepted by the Soviet. The Provisional Government, like the Tsar before it, was in the last resort obliged to rely upon the army for support.

Source B offers some support for the Provisional Government from the Conference of Soviets, but only if it fulfilled certain demands, such as working for peace and opposing counter-revolution. The implication is that this support might be withdrawn.

Source C displays outright hostility to the Government from an important opponent, Lenin, who sought to undermine it by propaganda, activity and a radical plan of reform.

The evidence of Sources D and E is more ambiguous: the implication is that Lenin did not immediately have everything his own way, but that he soon won support for his hostility to the Government.

However, these sources by themselves do not prove the statement that the Provisional Government was doomed to failure from the beginning. The sources do not tell us exactly how influential Lenin and the Soviet were in their demands; they do not tell us how the majority of the army and population responded; they do not tell us about later events such as the failure of the summer offensive and the Kornilov Revolt, which were influential in losing support for the Government. We can recognise from these sources the potential problems of the Provisional Government, but more evidence would be necessary before we could conclude with confidence that it was 'doomed to failure from the beginning of its existence.'

Approaching Essay Questions

The key to writing successful history essays must always be, in the last resort, the ability to achieve relevance. In other words, you must answer the particular question set. Relevance is worth much more than length or a mass of detail. Accurate knowledge is also important, but only if it is employed to back up a particular argument, not for its own sake. Un-analytical narrative, or prepared answers to a topic which do not meet the requirements of the particular title set, are probably the commonest failings of examination answers. Conversely, the best answers are often concise, always relevant, analytical, and show evidence of wide and thoughtful reading. Your command of the English language is not being tested as such, but you must be able to present your arguments effectively!

Plan your essays. Break the question down into its key components. What are the key phrases or words in the question? Give your essays a shape: an introduction which will introduce the main argument and possibly indicate how you hope to approach it; a logical main body, written in paragraphs (sometimes ignored by students!); and a conclusion which does not repeat the bulk of your essay but neatly draws together the threads. Other issues such as style and use of quotations are also important if you wish to write lucidly and well. As with most things in life, essay-writing usually improves with practice.

In most of the history essays you encounter, you will be asked to evaluate a statement or quotation. There are usually different approaches possible: therefore, 'model' answers must be treated with caution. It is, for example, quite in order to approach a controversial issue by considering evidence which supports different sides of an argument, without necessarily coming down decisively on one side of a particular interpretation. On the other hand, it is quite acceptable to argue a particular viewpoint, provided you can produce supporting evidence. Credit will usually be given if you show relevant knowledge of contemporary and/or more recent sources.

There are books available which deal in some depth with issues such as analytical reading, question analysis and essay-writing. Students may well find any of the following useful:

C. Brasher: *The Young Historian* (OUP 1970)

J. Cloake, V. Crinnon and S. Harrison: *The Modern History Manual* (Framework Press 1987)

J. Fines: *Studying to Succeed – History at 'A' Level and Beyond* (Longman 1986)

The following list of essay titles on Soviet History includes suggestions (no more than suggestions!) on how to approach them, plus a specimen answer. Use them as part of your course or for examination practice.

Possible Essay Titles

1 How valid is the view that the First World War rendered the overthrow of tsardom inevitable?

There are two main aspects to be considered here: first, how significant the war was in bringing about the March Revolution; and second, were there any factors beside the war that contributed to the overthrow of tsardom? Then it would be legitimate to assess the issue of 'possibility' and 'probability' as opposed to 'inevitability'.

Analysis of the role of the war might include the following: the change from early patriotic enthusiasm to growing disenchantment; military disaster; administrative, economic and fiscal problems; the role of the Tsar and other members of his regime; the attitudes of various social groupings – peasants, workers, middle class, intelligentsia, aristocracy; political manoeuvrings. Other issues might include: the limited role of the revolutionary parties between 1914 and 1917; a comparison with earlier crises such as the 1905 Revolution; and the whole historical debate as to the inherent stability of the tsarist regime on the eve of war.

What *must* be avoided is a narrative account of the war years and the February/March Revolution.

2 Do you agree with Trotsky's assertion that the March Revolution 'was led by politically-conscious workers educated for the most part by the party of Lenin'?

Different aspects of this question which need to be considered are: how 'politically conscious' were the workers? What part did Lenin's party play in 'educating' them? This should lead to a discussion of the Bolsheviks' influence amongst the proletariat and indeed the influence, if any, of other parties. The events of the March Revolution have to be considered and

95

possibly the varying interpretations of that event: was it essentially a spontaneous event or was it 'led' by a particular group or personality, regardless of the fact that workers were clearly involved?

3 Why did the power of the Provisional Government last for only eight months?

A straightforward question, but a narrative of 1917 should be avoided. A thorough answer should analyse: the weaknesses and problems facing the Government (for example, Dual Power); policies such as continuation of the war; the impact of specific events such as the July Days and the Kornilov Revolt; and the activities of opponents, particularly the Bolsheviks. Some overall analysis of the relative importance of these factors – both those within the Government's control and those outside its control – should be attempted, even though it may not be possible to reach a definitive conclusion.

4 How do you account for the apparent ease with which the Bolsheviks seized power in November 1917?

To some extent this may be treated as a variant on the question above. Certainly the role of the Provisional Government and its policies should be discussed; but also it is necessary to analyse the strengths and weaknesses of the various political groupings, including, of course, those of the Bolsheviks and their leaders, in order to attempt some overall assessment.

5 How valid is the statement that the Civil War 'undoubtedly had an enormous impact on the Bolsheviks and the young Soviet Republic'?

What must be avoided here is a narrative of the Civil War or an analysis of why the Bolsheviks won. You are being asked specifically about the *impact*: this includes the political – the impact upon the development of the Communist Party and its attitude towards dissent, for example; the economic – in part at least War Communism was a response to the pressures of war; and the psychological – the impact upon Communist attitudes ('isolationism' etc.).

The bulk of the answer will be concerned with the period up to 1921, but it would be legitimate also to consider any longer-term impact.

6 Why were the Bolsheviks' opponents unable to overthrow the Soviet regime between 1917 and 1921?

Another 'Civil War' question, but again it should be treated analytically rather than descriptively. A good answer should consider who exactly the various 'opponents' were, both internal and external, and what their strengths and weaknesses were. The strengths and weaknesses of the Bolsheviks themselves must be considered, with an assessment of their policies and reaction to them during this period. Some overall assessment which balances the relative strengths and weaknesses of both sides may be attempted.

7 Do you agree that War Communism represented 'an uneasy combination of utopian and practical elements'?

Whatever view you arrive at on this issue, it is essential to examine both aspects of the question. The 'utopian' element prompts an examination of the views of those Bolsheviks like Bukharin, who welcomed the measures of War Communism as the correct path to socialism and then communism. The 'practical' issue invites an examination of the somewhat haphazard way in which many of these measures were introduced, partly in response to economic difficulties and problems caused by war. Clearly, to answer this question well, you must have a detailed knowledge of the actual measures and some understanding of the views of the protagonists in the drama.

8 Assess the argument of a Soviet historian that 'The New Economic Policy strengthened the alliance between the workers and peasants and secured the victory of the socialist elements over the capitalist ones'.

This is quite a demanding question. To answer it thoroughly you must be secure in your knowledge of how and why the New Economic Policy was introduced. Then perhaps you should consider what exactly were the 'socialist elements' and what were the 'capitalist' ones. How far was the NEP (and for that matter its predecessor, War Communism) socialist, or capitalist, or a combination of both? What does the 'alliance between the workers and peasants' actually mean? An analysis of events in the early 1920s – such as the Scissors Crisis – may help you reach some conclusions about the statement.

9 Examine the significance of developments in the organisation of the Communist Party between the November Revolution and Lenin's death in 1924.

A straightforward question if you have studied this topic. The main developments should be described: the growth of the Party; the organisational changes such as the development of a central Party machine; the increasingly hierarchical and centralised nature of that machine; and specific events such as the 1921 Congress, with its ban on factionalism. Do not over-concentrate on the role of personalities, although some, like Stalin, are clearly important. Be sure to examine the *significance*: e.g. to what extent was Russia a monolithic one-party state by 1924? How far had Lenin's worries about 'bureaucratisation' been realised? What significance did these developments have for individuals like Trotsky and Stalin?

10 Examine the view that 'Lenin stood for the application of Marxism to the specifically Russian historical situation'.

An interesting question – but only if you know your theory! You must display some knowledge of the main tenets of Marxism and also of Leninism, if you are to consider the extent to which Lenin *did* accept Marx. Indeed, you should consider the issue of how far in fact Lenin was a pragmatist, prepared to act in whatever way appeared most fruitful in a particular situation – and what exactly was the 'specifically Russian historical situation'? Clearly this question involves a knowledge of both theory and practice, so do not neglect one at the expense of the other, but always relate the theory to the practice.

11 Was the struggle for power after Lenin's death motivated by personal rivalries or ideological differences?

A straightforward question, but beware: students often become so pre-occupied with the struggle between Stalin and the Left and Right oppositions and Stalin's supposed thirst for power that the role of ideology is downgraded. Ideological arguments *were* important; although there was agreement on the need for Russia to modernise and industrialise, there were fierce arguments about the best route to this goal. Therefore, some form of balanced assessment of the role of personality and ideology should be attempted.

12 Why did Trotsky's influence in Russia decline during the 1920s?

Try to avoid a pure narrative of Trotsky's career. An assessment of Trotsky's importance during the Revolution and Civil War is certainly called for, followed by the manoeuvrings for position at the time of Lenin's demise. The 1920s may be seen as a combination of Trotsky's mistakes and perhaps the strengths of his rivals, but attempt an assessment and avoid the trap of treating the question as a straight 'Stalin *versus* Trotsky' question.

13 Examine the view that, for Stalin, collectivisation was a political success but an economic disaster.

Remember that to judge successes and disasters, you need to consider the aims. Therefore establish what the aims of collectivisation were; then examine both the political and economic implications from *Stalin's* point of view (avoid long passages on the human misery of the peasantry, because although relevant, it is not the main point at issue here).

14 How successful was the First Five-Year Plan in achieving its aims?

(*See specimen answer on page 100*)

15 Assess the strength of the Soviet economy on the eve of war in 1941.

A straightforward question provided you do not fall into the trap of narrating the events of the Five-Year Plans. You are being asked to analyse the *effects* of the Plans and of collectivisation on the economy – not complicated, provided you have studied the topic in detail.

16 'Stalin's Terror combined sheer and arbitrary destructiveness with brutal political logic'. Do you agree?

Analyse the terms of the question carefully. First establish what Stalin's Terror actually was. How destructive was it? This is an interesting issue in itself if you consider it in terms of economic, human, and military cost. Then again, was it arbitrary or was it planned? Or did it begin as a planned exercise and then become arbitrary? Was there any logic? (Perhaps there was from Stalin's standpoint if no-one elses.) These are all issues which should be pursued – *not* a straight narrative of what happened during the Purges.

17 'Stalin's Russia represented a turning away from the socialist ideals of the October Revolution'. Is this a valid assessment?

Not an easy question unless you define your terms of reference carefully. You must define the 'socialist ideals' – whether you conceive of them in terms of orthodox Marxism or Marxism-Leninism. It is necessary to consider how well Stalin's Russia of the 1930s fits in with these theories, but you should also assess the intervening years: was Russia moving towards or away from socialism before Stalin implemented his policies? To answer this question thoroughly it would be helpful if you have some knowledge of contemporary and later critiques of Stalin, such as Trotsky's denunciations of Stalin's regime and theories of 'state capitalism'. It would also be legitimate to touch on the issue of how far Lenin was responsible for some of the trends which later became evident under Stalin.

18 How consistent was Soviet cultural policy between the Revolution and 1941?

This is a straightforward question *provided* you have studied culture in some detail. 'Culture' may be treated in a fairly broad sense to include education and religion as well as the arts. You should be aware of the Marxist-Leninist conception of culture and how the *relative* freedom of the 1920s gave way to the prescriptive interpretation of culture under Stalin.

19 Assess Soviet policy between 1917 and 1941 towards EITHER education OR the Church OR literature.

This is a variant on the question above, except that of course you must have detailed knowledge of *one* particular aspect of culture. Make sure that you *evaluate* Soviet policy as well as describe it.

20 Do historians attach more significance to personalities than ideas in the history of Soviet Russia?

These historiographical questions are rarely easy, but can be fruitful and interesting if approached carefully. With this question, consider particular aspects or themes of Soviet history (e.g. the struggle for power in the 1920s) and consider the significance of personalities and ideas. You must show acquaintance with at least some historical interpretations, preferably covering a spectrum of opinion, if you are to do justice to the question.

21 How objective have historians been in their interpretation of Soviet history between 1917 and 1941?

As with the question above, a good answer *must* show knowledge of historians' work, and cannot be a mere account of events. It is advisable to have studied a range of sources and historians, including some Soviet ones if possible.

Specimen Essay Answer

(See page 98)

The answer below is not a model answer, nor does it necessarily represent the only approach. Nevertheless, it is an answer which focuses on the question and does represent the type of answer which may be written under examination conditions, in about 45 minutes.

How successful was the First Five-Year Plan in achieving its aims?

It should have been no surprise when the First Five-Year Plan was launched in the USSR in 1928. After all, modernisation and industrialisation of the country had been on the agenda since the Revolution, and indeed were seen as integral to the development of socialist and ultimately communist society.

The delay in implementing a programme of rapid industrialisation may be attributed to several factors: among them the 'temporary retreat' of NEP in the face of the apparently intractable economic difficulties of the post-revolutionary period; a shortage of expertise and money; and the (at times) bitter arguments within the Party. These arguments were not over the goal of industrialisation, which was accepted as axiomatic, but over the methods of achieving that goal – hence the arguments over the issue of whether the peasants should be 'enriched' or 'squeezed' in order to finance industry. Such opposing views had been reflected in the political manoeuvrings which culminated in Stalin's defeat of the Right opposition in 1929.

What were the aims of the First Five-Year Plan? The obvious answer would be to say that the principal aim was to transform Russia into a modern industrial state, since in Stalin's opinion 'We are fifty or a hundred years behind the advanced countries. We must make good this distance in ten years. Either we do it, or we shall be crushed.'

However, the actual implementation of the Plan was a complex matter. It was one thing for the Communists to agree on a radical system of long-term planning and allocation of resources by the state, but there was no blueprint from which to work. There was very little in either the Marxist or Leninist canon – apart from a few ringing but largely meaningless slogans like 'Soviets plus electrification equals Communism' – from which the planners could formulate practical suggestions as opposed to ideological inspiration. There were no other planned economies which could point the way ahead. All that the planners had to guide them was the limited experience of a few major projects already undertaken before 1928, such as the Turksib railway and certain hydro-electric power projects, and some theoretical plans drawn up by Gosplan, the planning organisation.

In reality therefore, the targets set in 1928 were arbitary, and there was an 'optimistic' and a 'realistic' version of the Plan in terms of expectations. However, even the 'realistic' version made some unrealistic assumptions about, for example, increases in labour productivity. Targets were altered while the Plan was in progress.

The Plan was declared complete in 1932, nine months ahead of schedule. It is dangerous to make dogmatic assertions about the physical achievements of the Plan: estimates and available statistics vary considerably according to the sources used. Nevertheless, it can be confidently said that there were some remarkable achievements: the construction of vast projects such as the Dnieper dam; rapid strides in certain industries such as engineering; and large increases in fuel output. Some of the more outlying areas of the USSR received industrial investment for the first time.

Production of consumer goods did not rise rapidly, but since they were given a low priority in the Plan compared to heavy industry, this cannot be considered a failure.

Unemployment was eliminated and indeed there was a labour shortage. However, labour productivity was low, partly because many of the new workforce were former peasants, slow to adapt to new working methods. There was also a high labour turnover. Mistakes were made by planners, managers and operatives.

Overall, the Plan might be deemed an economic success in that it laid an infrastructure which was to be utilised in the Second Plan in 1933. Although labour productivity was low, the USSR was well on the way to becoming the second greatest industrial power in the world – certainly one of Stalin's intentions – and Russia had avoided most of the problems of the world depression. Russia's survival against Germany in the Second World War was at least partly due to these developments.

The fact that labour productivity grew at a slower rate than gross national product implies that increases in production were due mainly to the Russian people working harder, plus the influx of peasants and women into the workforce. Also, from 1931 Stalin denounced the principle of egalitarianism and allowed the use of incentives.

There was a decline in living standards and the quality of life generally, reflected in shortages of consumer goods and poor housing in the overcrowded cities. However, this cannot be considered a failure since Stalin had always maintained that sacrifices were necessary if heavy industry was to be developed in the long run. Indeed, from Stalin's standpoint, the fact that resources were released for the industrialisation drive at the expense of living standards would have been regarded as a success.

Stalin in fact had achieved his stated aim of 'Socialism in one country' (although of course this depends to some extent upon one's interpretation of 'socialism') partly by milking the peasants in the way his Left-wing opponents had advocated in the 1920s!

So far I have concentrated on economic factors. However, there were political and psychological implications also. Stalin had proved that he was the master. His control over the Party and the Party's hold over the country were enhanced. A mass of fresh, young Party members came to the fore, devoted to the Stalinist ideal and ready to form the new élite of 'working-class intellectuals'. They were to replace the old guard. In this sense the Purges were related to the Five-Year Plans. It is no coincidence that the Seventeenth Congress of 1934 was labelled the 'Congress of Victors' as the Party congratulated itself on its success.

To conclude therefore: in human terms, particularly for the peasants but also for the urban work force, the processes of the First Five-Year Plan were harsh and in many cases disastrous. In purely statistical terms there were great achievements and also failures. But in terms of Stalin's ultimate objective, that of laying the foundations of a great industrial power and reinforcing his own position, the First Five-Year Plan must be labelled a success. Stalin continued what Peter the Great and Witte had begun, but Stalin operated on a much larger scale; and Stalin's success was such that his system of economic planning was regarded as a model for many other undeveloped economies. The Stalinist system has only relatively recently come under questioning in the USSR – and is proving to be a complex and dangerous task to dismantle.

BIBLIOGRAPHY

This bibliography is not exhaustive. Extensive bibliographies may be found in many books and monographs on Soviet History. Nevertheless the books that have been listed below are those that should be reasonably accessible to students and teachers, and they are available in paperback format.

E. H. Carr: *The History of Soviet Russia* (Penguin. First published 1950). Carr's *magnum opus*, unrivalled in scope and detail, but to be used probably as a reference work. Carr tends to concentrate on the evolution of institutions and laws, perhaps to the neglect of personalities and the ordinary people, who rarely figure at all! More accessible is Carr's one-volume summary *The Russian Revolution From Lenin To Stalin 1917–29* (Penguin 1979).

T. Cliff: *Lenin* (3 volumes, Bookmarks 1987). A very readable, detailed account by a socialist historian of Lenin and the events in Russia during his lifetime. Particularly useful is the inclusion of a considerable quantity of primary source material and some interesting analysis.

R. Conquest: *The Harvest of Sorrow* (OUP 1987). This book has attracted some criticism for its approach towards the 'terror famine', but nevertheless is a very detailed account of the tragedy of collectivisation between 1929 and 1933, dealing with background, motives, effects and responsibilities.

R. Conquest: *The Great Terror* (Penguin 1971). An extremely thorough account of all aspects of the Purges of the 1930s, and still probably indispensable for students investigating this particular topic in depth.

S. Fitzpatrick: *The Russian Revolution 1917–1932* (OUP 1982). A readable account and analysis treating the years 1917–1932 as essentially successive steps in one important process – the Russian Revolution. A mixture of narrative and thoughtful analysis, it provides a useful overview of several important issues, although it needs to be complemented by more specialised books for students studying the topic in depth.

G. Hosking: *A History of The Soviet Union* (Fontana 1985). A recommended general textbook. It covers some often neglected aspects such as religion and nationality. Should be used with more specialised texts.

P. Kenez: **The Birth Of The Propaganda State** (CUP 1985). A readable and very informative account of the role of propaganda in the 1920s, covering the press, education, the youth movement, the cinema, and censorship. The book deals not just with official policy but with the actual impact of propaganda on ordinary people. There is no adequate substitute in English, and we await a similar exposition of propaganda in the 1930s.

W. Laquer: *The Fate Of The Revolution* (Collier 1987). First published over 20 years ago, this study has still not been surpassed as a broad survey of interpretations of Soviet history from 1917 to the present day. Particularly useful for students of historiography, it surveys interpretations of 1917, views for and against Lenin and Stalin, and a survey of western and Soviety historiography right up to the 1980s.

M. Liebmann: *Leninism Under Lenin* (Merlin Press 1975). A sympathetic account of Lenin, both as a revolutionary theorist and activist before 1917, as a revolutionary leader in 1917, and as a post-revolutionary statesman. There is also an analysis of Leninist Russia and relations between revolutionary Russia and the outside workd. This is not an easy book, but is useful in a discussion of issues such as the nature of Lenin's achievements, deficiencies, and responsibility or otherwise for later events.

E. Mawdsley: *The Russian Civil War* (Allen and Unwin 1987). Clearly and concisely written, and the only easily accessible one-volume objective account of the subject, this is strongly recommended for students investigating issues such as the role of Allied intervention and the part played by various individuals. Particularly valuable is the conclusion which debates the issue of how far the Whites 'lost' the war and to what extent the Reds 'won' it; and the cost to Russia.

M. McCauley: *Stalin And Stalinism* (Longman Seminar Studies in History 1983). The first two sections, on the 1920s and 1930s, are relevant. The collection of documents is hardly exhaustive, but the detailed introduction, assessing the main issues of those years, is lucid and valuable.

M. McCauley: *The Soviet Union Since 1917* (Longman 1981). A readable introduction to some of the main issues and events in Soviet history, to be read in conjunction with more specialised works.

A. Nove: *An Economic History Of The USSR* (Penguin 1969). Still very authoritative and probably unrivalled as a concise but detailed survey of the theory and practice of the Soviet economy. Should certainly be read by students studying the Soviet economy between 1917 and 1941.

A. Rybakov: *Children Of The Arbat* (Arrow 1989). There are many illuminating novels concerned with this period. I recommend this one: a seminal novel, suppressed for many years in the USSR, it successfully fuses the story of a group of young Muscovites in the early 1930s with a psychological portrait of Stalin preparing to unleash the Great Terror. Very good on the atmosphere and illogicality of the Terror.

A. Solzhenitsyn: *The Gulag Archipelago* (abridged ed. Collins Harvill 1988). A vivid and personal account of Stalin's convict empire, collated from many who suffered directly.

N. Sukhanov: *The Russian Revolution 1917* (abridged in one volume. Princeton University Press 1984). Originally a 7-volume history of the period between the two revolutions of 1917. Sukhanov was originally an SR, later a Menshevik. His book was written in 1922 and was later suppressed by Stalin. It has the advantages and drawbacks of a contemporary account, but overall it is a reasonably balanced one and it is probably the best of contemporary accounts in terms of its dramatic and fresh qualities.

A. Wood: *The Russian Revolution* (Longman Seminar Studies 1986). As with McCauley's collection on Stalin, useful less for its collection of sources than for its detailed and analytical introduction which considers all the major issues, beginning with an analysis of political groupings in Russia at the turn of the century and ending with the economic strategies of War Communism and NEP.

Films

Some classic Soviet films of the 1920s and 1930s are commercially available and provide a useful supplement to other sources as well as providing an insight into propaganda and film techniques.

The best examples are Eisenstein's classics: *Strike*, *Battleship Potemkin*, and *October*. His *Ivan The Terrible* provides an ironic commentary on Stalinism.

Pudovkin's *End Of St. Petersburg* provides an interesting contrast with *October* in its account of the October Revolution.

INDEX